Henry Dufton

Narrative of a Journey Through Abyssinia in 1862-3

Henry Dufton

Narrative of a Journey Through Abyssinia in 1862-3

ISBN/EAN: 9783337011093

Printed in Europe, USA, Canada, Australia, Japan

Cover: Foto ©Andreas Hilbeck / pixelio.de

More available books at **www.hansebooks.com**

NARRATIVE

OF

A JOURNEY THROUGH ABYSSINIA

In 1862–3.

SECOND EDITION.

LONDON:
CHAPMAN & HALL, 193, PICCADILLY.
1867.

PREFACE.

My object in undertaking the journey into Africa, a portion of which is described in the following narrative, was to reach the Galla countries to the south of Abyssinia, and explore, as a field for Christianisation and future colonisation, the healthy highlands which native reports lead us to believe exist in that part of the African continent.

This I intended doing either by way of the White Nile and Sobat, or the Blue Nile and Didhessa. The latter was the one ultimately chosen; but having been robbed in the Bahiouda desert, and detained three months in Sennaar by the rains, I was at length obliged to relinquish the undertaking for the time being, and seek an outlet for home. I thus proposed the journey through Abyssinia.

As the general interest is now engaged in Abyssinia, I have thought it desirable, in order not to delay the reader, to start at Khartoum. I had already prepared a few chapters on the journey through Dongola and the Bahiouda desert to Khartoum; but these, at the wish of my publishers and for the reason above stated, I have suppressed. This explanation is necessary to account for the abruptness with which the narrative begins.

Not imagining that Abyssinia and its affairs would so soon assume importance, I took no notes on the journey; but, on arrival at Aden, I gave my friends at home a brief account of my experiences; and this, enlarged by fresh draughts on memory, I now present to the public.

In the Appendix on the Abyssinian Question I have endeavoured to give a brief story of the captivity, and have also tried to present a view of the difficulties our expedition will have to encounter in the invasion of Theodore's territory. I have also given my views as to the most practicable route for an army to reach his territory; but as I have no experience in military matters, I feel it behoves me to speak with diffidence on such subjects.

The map of Abyssinia, which faces the Title-page, is for the most part constructed from Dr. Beke's, and is given principally with the object of showing my route. The colouring is intended to distinguish between fertile (green) and desert (yellow) country; where water is abundant, and where it is scarce.

The sketch maps of my own route are simply drawn from memory, and consequently do not pretend to any great degree of accuracy; but I think they are truthful as far as giving a general idea of the country passed through.

HENRY DUFTON.

STREATHAM, *September* 26, 1867.

CONTENTS.

CHAPTER I.

KHARTOUM TO MESELEMIEH.

CHAPTER II.

MESELEMIEH TO WAD MEDINEH.

CHAPTER III.

WAD MEDINEH TO MATAMMAH.

CHAPTER IV.

MATAMMAH TO TCHELGA.

CHAPTER V.

TCHELGA TO GAFFAT.

CHAPTER VI.

GAFFAT.

CHAPTER VII.

DEBRA TABOR.

CHAPTER VIII.

DEBRA TABOR.

CHAPTER VIII (*continued.*)

DEBRA TABOR.

CHAPTER IX.

DEBRA TABOR.

CHAPTER X.

WOFFERGHEF.

CHAPTER XI.

DEBRA TABOR TO ADOWA.

CHAPTER XII.

ADOWA TO MASSOWAH.

CHAPTER XIII.

MASSOWAH TO ADEN.

APPENDIX.

THE ABYSSINIAN CAPTIVES QUESTION.

NARRATIVE

OF

A JOURNEY THROUGH ABYSSINIA.

CHAPTER I.

KHARTOUM TO MESELEMIEH.

Departure from Khartoum—Myself and my donkey—Uncomfortable
quarters—Arab greed—In the mud—A fellow-traveller—El Islam
in the Soudan—The Blue River—Tropical rains—Scorpions for
bedfellows—The Nuba tribes and Nubia—Experiences with my
donkey—Kamnin—Rich fertility of the country—Arab hospitality—-Adam's knife and fork—Amazons of East Africa—
Arrival at Meselemieh.

AFTER about a month's stay at Khartoum, I began to
think it time to move. The season was too late for boats
to proceed up the Blue River, so I had to adopt the
land route along its banks, and this I thought I might
well do on foot; but as I still had a great weight of
baggage, I was obliged to purchase a donkey for its

B

conveyance. These arrangements completed, and the animal loaded, I turned my face again southwards. I was blown out of Khartoum in the same manner that I had been blown into it, for the rainy season, which was now (July) about setting in, is here always heralded by slight tornadoes. In order to cut a corner off I struck out at once into the desert which surrounds Khartoum, driving my donkey before me. There was no path, but I thought I knew sufficiently the direction I ought to take to insure my not leaving the river at too great a distance. After advancing for some time, the approach of evening made me begin to fear that if I persisted in cutting off corners I might not arrive at a village before dark, so I turned towards a clump of trees in the distance, where I knew the river must be, and after about an hour reached the village of Gereff on its banks. Having got a man to assist me in unloading my donkey, I tied him to a tree, and then spread out my straw mat on the ground, and arranged the two cufas (panniers) at either end.

After a supper of bread and milk, I lay down for the night; but had scarcely got into my first doze, when I was awakened by the consciousness of feeling remarkably cold and uncomfortable. After dreamily arguing the matter in my own mind as to what it could possibly be which made me feel so uneasy, I at last came to the conclusion that it was neither more nor less than rain. When I had satisfied myself of the fact, my first move was to get underneath the bed, and this I managed by turning my straw mat into a coverlet, and lying down in the place where the bed ought to be. Not many coverlets, even when half an inch thick, as mine was, will stand torrents of rain, and the water soon appeared inside. I then made a move towards the side of a house a little sheltered from the wet, and had the cruelty to displace a number of goats quietly ensconced there, as I thought "the claims of humanity" the best. This, however, was of no avail, for it rained more heavily there than anywhere, considering that each drop had a large proportion of mud in it, gathered from the dusty roof. I now sought shelter elsewhere, but found none; so after wandering about more than half the night, I *coolly* waited till morning.

I spent part of the next day at the village, for the ground was too soft to proceed, and shot a few pigeons for the benefit of the man who entertained me. This fellow had an eye to business, and wanted to do a little barter with his Franjee visitor. In the first place, he wished to exchange his old knocked-up donkey for my own. As I had been taken in once with my donkey, he having what they call *ahboob* (which experience interpreted to me as short-winded), I thought I would keep clear of another worse bargain. He then offered me an old female slave, in constitution very much like his donkey. He asked £1 for her, which, were it not that the poor creature was minus teeth, and had one foot in the grave, was perhaps not dear.

In the afternoon I recommenced my journey, as the heat of the sun had dried up the road somewhat. Towards evening I came to the village of Soba; but when within a mile of it my poor fellow-traveller had the misfortune to stick in the mud, and, finding he could not extricate himself, quietly composed his limbs under him, and lay down. This was very awkward for me, for by myself I could not get the load on to his back again, and there was nobody near to assist me. Moreover, the shades of night were drawing on, so there was nothing for it but to make up my mind to stop there. I fastened the poor beast to a bush, placed my baggage at the head of my bed, and my gun at my side, and lay down to sleep, not awaking till daylight.

Next day I was overtaken by an old Arab from

Berber, whom, as he was travelling the same way as myself, and well acquainted with the road and people, I was very glad to join. At noon I had an interesting conversation with some Arabs, with whom we stayed during the midday heat. They wished me to repeat the Mohammedan creed, *La illah ila Allah wa Mohammed er-rasool Allah.* "There is no god but God," said I, and then stopped. "And Mohammed is the prophet of God," continued they. "That I cannot say," I replied, "for I don't believe Mohammed was the prophet of God." They were greatly shocked at this infidel sentiment, and commenced to argue the question in a manner pretty similar to that in which most persons at home would argue for the truths of Christianity—namely, by heaping assertion on assertion. I asked them when I saw their bigotry of what religion they would have been had they been born in Europe, where all are Christians, or in Central Africa, where all are heathens, in neither of which countries do the generality of people know anything of Mohammed and his doctrines. They were silent, and only one granted he would have been what he had been brought up to. I went farther, and told them to refer back to their own past history when they were heathens, and how they became Mohammedans; and, to refresh their memory, said that when the sword was at their throat, and they were told to say *La illah*, &c., or die, they preferred to live, and said it; and that if the French, who had once got a footing in Egypt, had come as far as to them and spread Christianity at the edge of the sword, they would have turned Christians also. I said, " You know nothing about the Holy Book of the Christians, and yet you condemn me as a *kafer* and Nazarene dog for believing in it; what you've to do is to compare the Kitab el Makudus (Bible) with the Koran, and seek for the truth; this I have done for myself, and believe the Christian to be the superior religion." They really assume to believe in the Bible, stating however that we have corrupted it. They often repeat a verse, including what they consider the four holy books:

Et Toorat betaa Moosa	. . .	The Law of Moses.
El Muzmoor betaa Daood	. . .	The Psalms of David.
El Engeel betaa Eesa	. . . .	The Gospel of Jesus.
El Koran betaa Mohammed	. .	The Koran of Mohammed.

They say that the prophet whom Moses said "the Lord God would raise up like to himself" was En-Nebee Mohammed. I have asked them sometimes whom they consider greatest, Jesus or Mohammed. Most have said Mohammed, but some few say Jesus. They believe that Jesus will come at the end of this age, and destroy the Christians and heathen, but spare and bless the Moslemeen. They also believe in a great persecutor of the Mohammedans to arise in the latter day, whom Christ is to destroy at His coming. They hate the Jews much more than the Christians, though Judaism approaches much nearer El Islam than Christianity can do. I was much amused by one who asserted that the ourang-outangs were a tribe of Jews who had been changed by the Almighty into that shape for their unbelief. This is rather reversing Darwin's theory.

The banks of the Blue Nile are richly clothed with vegetation. The land is much cultivated, the produce supporting a dense population as well as supplying Khartoum and other markets. Doura or maize is the principal cereal.

The rainy season seemed now to have fully set in, and scarcely a day would pass without a heavy shower. In one of these we were caught when we were within a quarter of a mile from a house; but nothing would induce the donkeys to face the pelting storm, which was blown from the direction in which we were proceeding. Immense numbers of small locusts were driven by the wind into our faces, which, with the heavy rain, made us as well as our beasts glad to seek the shelter of some trees. We unloaded the donkeys, and squatted down behind the baggage, covering ourselves with the large straw mat. The storm, however, did not abate, so that we were completely soaked ; the water running down us even filled our shoes. But with whatever amount of fortitude we put up with our lot, we could not compare it with the stoic endurance of our beasts. Twitching their four legs up underneath their bellies in a manner which put one in mind of the conjuror's goat standing on the neck of a bottle, and tucking their tails in between their hind legs, they turned their backs to the storm, and never budged throughout the whole of its continuance, though it lasted more than an hour. The extensive plain over which we had been proceeding appeared like one vast lake, and objects at the shortest distance were perfectly concealed from view by the descending torrents. Upon its ceasing, the old man, who was a woodsman, drew out a hatchet, and began getting at the dry interior of a decayed tree near at hand, with which we had soon made a good roaring fire, that enabled us to dry our clothes and procure a good hot cup of coffee. By drying the wet branches of the trees near the fire we had sufficient fuel to keep it alive all night, for we had made up our minds to sleep there, the donkeys not being able to walk in the mud. I slept soundly enough, but scarcely should have done so had I known what I found out in the morning—that three scorpions had been my bed-fellows. The largest was an ugly fellow four inches long, and I found him in the very folds of my blanket. We found the road very bad after the rain, and I often had to walk barefoot in the mud. This was better than continually leaving your shoe at the bottom of a deep hole, and being obliged to fish it out with your hand.

We passed in succession the villages of Gedid, Nuba, Masid, and Eltie. Gedid, like many other Newtowns (for such it means) which could be mentioned, seems now getting pretty old. It has a market twice a week. The name of Nuba is possibly a relic of the great Nuba people, who gave the name of Nubia to the country south of Egypt, the remains of whom in addition to the present inhabitants of that country may also probably be traced in the Nuba, who now occupy a small tract opposite Sennaar, and the Noba or Nuba tribes to the south of Kordofan. Masid and Eltie have semi-weekly markets, and the former contains a mosque.

At Eltie I bade good-bye to my companion, after having been five days in his company. I had now to proceed alone, and had occasion the next evening to wish my old friend with me again, for my donkey took it into his head, though we were near a village, to cry "Hold, enough!" and squat down in the middle of a dark wood. Though no doubt very wrong, I must confess that on such occasions I was strongly inclined to indulge in Macbeth's charitable wish on him who should utter the above exclamation, and I even did vent my wrath in a few expletives in the animal's native Arabic. I was thus compelled again to sleep out of doors; but this I should not have minded had not the people now begun to talk of lions and hyenas, which made me feel somewhat timid. Fear, however, eventually gave way to sleep, and I was told next morning that my apprehensions had been groundless, for there were no wild animals in that neighbourhood.

The succeeding day I reached Kamnin, the largest and most important place since leaving Khartoum. A great quantity of soap is manufactured here, which is much cheaper than the European quality, but not so good.

As I proceeded I began to perceive a marked change

in the nature of the vegetation which clothes the side of the river. A greater variety of trees with long creeping cactus plants hanging from their branches, and a corresponding greater number and variety of birds, now took the place of the general desolation of the lower Nile countries; and as the occasional storms of thunder and lightning only tended to make the air cooler and more salubrious, I began now to enjoy my walk with as great a relish as if it had been along the banks of the Rhine instead of within the tropics. I took it very easy in this district, seldom doing more than ten miles a day. The only drawback was the incorrigible nature of my donkey, who would persist in continually lying down in the middle of the road, sometimes making me wait an hour or two for some passer-by to help me reload again.

On leaving Kamnin I got into the wrong path, which took me into the middle of a wood almost impenetrable from the closeness of the thorny trees. But this was not the worst, for in addition the soil was so soft we could scarcely proceed, and in the end the poor beast sank down the whole length of his legs; I literally had to dig him out. Finding I could not proceed by that route, I returned to the nearest village and

spent the night there. I never had any difficulty in
finding accommodation at any of these villages, for
Arab hospitality is proverbial. Indeed, there is in most
of them a hut set apart for this very purpose, in which
every wayfaring man is at liberty to stay as long as he
may think proper. In some of them a number of white
boards are hung up, on which persons who have passed
any time there signify the same and testify their gratitude. I was so pleased with the custom that I could
not forbear on one occasion doing the same, and wrote
a few words to the following effect in Arabic :

"Henry Dufton, a Christian *fakeer* (poor traveller),
spent one night here. He renders thanks to God for
the existence of such houses as these."

Not only is accommodation thus kindly given, but
the simple food of the people is also freely granted.
It generally consists of a kind of porridge, called
lukmeh, made of doura flour, which is served in a
wooden bowl. Over it is poured a thick sticky sauce,
made from *melookyeh* or *barmieh*, in which occasionally
a little meat is found. The latter is generally goat's
flesh dried in the sun, and afterwards rubbed into a
powder. With the very poorest these additions are luxu-
ries, and the *lukmeh* is only seasoned by salt dissolved

in warm water. The bowl in which it is placed stands in the middle of the floor, and around it squat the whole company, whose first movement is to tuck up the sleeve; the second, to plunge the hand into the soft mass; the third, to bring it out full; the fourth, to form what they have taken out into a large pellet; and the fifth, to drop that pellet into the mouth. Then, *da capo*. I at first had some difficulty in acquitting my-self honourably in these exercises, and my awkwardness would sometimes induce a smile from the rest; but practice soon makes perfect. On the whole, however, when I could purchase bread or milk I much pre-ferred it. I was not particular what kind of milk it might be — cow's, goat's, or camel's, all came in acceptable.

The following day my road lay in the direction of a place called Hellewain (literally " two villages "), and I passed on the road another, called Eftah el bâb (Open the door). As there was to be a market at the former I overtook many women proceeding to make purchases, who carried each a long double-edged sword, in order to protect themselves against robbers on the way. Few persons in these parts travel without some means of defence, and with the villagers the weapons generally consist of a long gun or sword. They wear also a small knife on the arm, just above the elbow, though this is rather for convenience than protection. The arms of the wandering Arabs are the spear and shield, and a group of these people form a very interesting sight to an European. On one occasion, not succeeding in reaching a village before dark, I spent the night in one of their encampments. It was in a retired part of a wood, and consisted of a number of black tents, which contained also their wives and families. I believe they lead this life here in order to avoid Turkish taxation. They are breeders of camels.

The above means of protection are not the only ones carried by the people. They put much confidence in the value of charms, which generally consist in portions of the Koran, fastened up in small rolls of leather and suspended on the neck and arms. Little children have sometimes large bunches dangling from their necks, which would probably weigh a pound or two. They say, moreover, that if water is made to pass over these portions of the Koran, and afterwards drunk, it will dispel disease. I saw one man who had met with an accident, and he attributed it all to his having left his charms at home.

A fortnight after my departure from Khartoum I reached Meselemieh, and here determined to stay and rest a little, if only for the benefit of Neddy. It was with some difficulty I engaged a house, there being very few in the town to let, and then I had to pay rather exorbitantly. I took it only for ten days; but the rains having now commenced in earnest, I was obliged to stay here twenty before I could get an opportunity of proceeding.

CHAPTER II.

MESELEMIEH, though from its being a comparatively
modern town it is not marked in most maps, is certainly,
after Khartoum, the most important place in Gezireh
Soudan; much more so than Wad Medineh or Sennaar.
It contains a population of probably 20,000, possesses
a mosque, and has a market the largest of its kind
in the neighbourhood. It is situated about four miles
from the Blue River, in the midst of a flat country,
consisting of a black vegetable soil. Some of the houses
are built of sun-dried bricks and have flat roofs, but
most of them are conical thatched huts. The latter are

made in the following manner:—In the first place a circle of about twenty feet diameter is described on the ground and surrounded by strong posts, each a yard apart, which are interlaced with thin pliable branches of trees, the whole being covered outwardly with doura stalks, tied together with the long grass common on the banks of the river. The roof is formed in skeleton on the ground. A number of beams, corresponding to that of the posts, are made to converge at the top, and are held in this position by concentric circles of plaited twigs; the whole being then raised to its position on the house, where it is fastened and made ready to receive the thatch of straw and grass. Not a nail or rivet of any kind is used in the construction of these buildings, and they are rendered totally impervious to the wet. Of course their disadvantage in comparison with mud houses is their liability to catch fire, one or two cases of which I have witnessed; but they are generally built at sufficient distance not to endanger others, and a house of this description is rebuilt in a day or two.

The roofs of these houses are in very many instances occupied by storks, who form their nests round the apex. I have often been interested in watching these birds when, coming from the river where they have been in search of food, they are greeted by their cackling young ones as they descend on to their curious perch. The people never molest them. The whole district abounds also with vultures; outside every town hundreds of them may be seen perched on the carcases of camels or donkeys; and it is not uncommon in the market-place for these birds to descend within a foot of your nose, and, seizing some refuse which may lie at your feet, mount up again into the air. Were it not for the vulture, the hyena, and the wolfish dog of these countries, the carelessness and uncleanliness of the people would inevitably result in bringing about the plague. These creatures are the only scavengers.

Notwithstanding their great services, Meselemieh is very unhealthy. This is principally owing to the flat nature of the country and its thickness of alluvial soil, which retains in a great measure the decayed vegetable matter resulting from heavy rains. During the wet season the town stands, as it were, in a complete lake; and I have actually had to wade ankle-deep, for a quarter of a mile, in proceeding to the market. There are also in the town many large pits, excavated for the clay wherewith to make bricks; they become the receptacle of all kinds of filth, not excluding the carcases of dogs, donkeys, horses, &c., which the wretched laziness of the people induces to cast in here rather than proceed a few yards farther to the outskirts of the town. Near the house in which I was residing there was one of this description, which might have a depth of fifty feet, but was for the most part dry on my arrival. A few days after, however, on the increase of the rains, the large receptacle was filled with water, so as to form a lake of 100 yards in width, in which were floating numbers of dead carcases; and when eventually the continuance of the rains made it overflow, the stench thus carried in different directions was fearful. Hitherto I had enjoyed the very best of health, not having had even the slightest indisposition, but now I began to feel the evil effects of the unhealthy atmosphere, which showed themselves in diarrhœa and general prostration of strength.

The country around Meselemieh is admirably adapted for the growth of the doura, yielding two crops in the year. While coming along I had noticed the peculiar way in which this is sown. A man goes before, holding by a long handle a narrow wooden spade, that at every other step he digs in the ground, at the same time giving it a sudden twist which forms a hole, in which two or

three grains of doura are dropped by a little girl who
follows, and who directly after closes it up with her foot.
The whole is performed very adroitly, and an entire
field may be thus sown in a very short space of time.

Some photographic portraits and picture books, as
well as a concertina I had with me, by them called
shaitan, or the devil, were a great source of amusement
to the people in my immediate neighbourhood, who,
especially the children, would beset the house in crowds,
and I was frequently invited out by my neighbours to a
booza-drinking. But I was particularly amused when,
on one occasion, my landlady came to me with a very
earnest request that I would play for the benefit of
another of her sex, whom she had brought with her.
" Why," I said, " what makes you so particularly desire
it?" "Oh," she replied, "this lady *fee wallad fil batnha*
(is enceinte), and in our country we believe that in such
cases music has a beneficial effect." With this powerful
inducement I put the instrument on at high pressure,
and I hope effectually.

My continued ill-health did not prevent me from
pursuing my journey as soon as a temporary cessation
of the rains would permit, and when I thought the
weather had cleared up a little, I again saddled my ass

and turned his face south. I had not proceeded far when I found myself on a road where the difficulties which opposed my animal's progress thickened in proportion to the thickness of the mud through which he had to make his way. I had got to a certain part of the road, where a man was holding by the horns a bull half mad with having spent the whole of the night up to his neck in a bog, when I was overtaken by a very respectable old sheik, on a well-conditioned donkey, the former of whom I had become acquainted with in Meselemieh, he having visited me to hear me read the Bible. He told me that I ought to have chosen another road, and advised me to retrace my steps for that purpose. This I was proceeding to do when my most unfortunate ass dropped once more. The old sheik, who was a few paces in front, hearing the squash, without turning his head said in an undertone to him having hold of the bull: " Is that his donkey that's gone down ?" " Yes," said the man ; whereupon the old gentleman dug his heels into the sides of the enviable beast he bestrode, and left the European to do what he could with his most troublesome donkey. That unfortunate individual now began to ask assistance from his companion the cowherd, who most sensibly said, "How can I let go the bull?" The whole scene was certainly very ludicrous. I sat down and waited till some passers-by came to my assistance.

That evening I reached the village of Tyibeh, the residence of the sheik of the district, Mohammed en-Nil. I was exceedingly well received by him, who came out to meet me with a bowl of sugared water, and, instead of the hut allotted in general for travellers, ordered his people to supply me with a house to myself, and with whatever food I should require. They wished my acceptance of a damsel of seventeen. I declined with thanks, alleging as my reason that Christians did not allow what Mohammedans permitted. They marvelled at the reply, and the maid likewise.

A day or two after I arrived at Wad Medineh, not, however, before I had again stuck fast, and had been compelled on the last day to engage a camel. If any of my friends want a lesson of patience, I can recommend to them nothing better than to drive a donkey afflicted with *ahboob* through the tropics during the rainy season.

I now began to see that it was totally impossible to proceed farther, and that I must make up my mind to pass the rainy season at Wad Medineh. I took a house, therefore, by the month, and quietly settled down for a stay.

Wad Medineh, situated on the left bank of the Blue River, was anciently, during the Sennaar dynasties, a place of great extent and importance. This is shown by the immense quantity of ruins which meet the eye on every side. During the administration of the Turks, however, it, as well as Sennaar the capital of the district, has sunk into comparative insignificance. The population was estimated to me as 10,000, but I should think my informant much overstated it. The soil being sandy and the ground undulating, it does not retain the wet so much as the country around Meselemieh—consequently it is esteemed more healthy. For the same reason, however, it is not so well adapted for cultivation; hence the surpassing importance Meselemieh has assumed, situated as it is in the midst of a vast doura district. Wad Medineh possesses barracks for the accommodation of a few hundred Turkish soldiers; also a bazaar and a mosque.

The celebrated kingdom of Sennaar is now a matter of the past, living only in the recollection of some of the older inhabitants. It once extended from the neighbourhood of Kordofan to the shores of the Red

Sea, and from Fazogl on the south to the confines of Egypt on the north. This immense country has been, since the time of Mohammed Ali, wholly in possession of the Turks, or, to speak more correctly, has become a tributary of the Egyptian government. The subjection of the natives was not brought about without a fierce struggle, that in some outlying districts is even now maintained; and even those who have submitted still bear a deep hate against their oppressors. It was the knowledge of their aversion which partly induced the King of Abyssinia to send his threatening message to the Pasha of Egypt, stating that as Emperor of Ethiopia he had a right to the dominions of his ancestors—meaning thereby Sennaar and even Dongola. I cannot think, however, that though the natives hate the Turks, they would prefer a Christian sovereign in their stead. I once heard a native of these parts utter a devout wish that God would extirpate the whole Makada, as they here term the Abyssinian nation. The event of an Abyssinian invasion was, nevertheless, considered sufficiently probable to induce the despatch of Musa Pasha from Cairo with an army of 10,000, whose daily arrival was expected at Khartoum while I was there.

The rains were scarcely so formidable as I had

imagined; for though it was manifest by the sky that there was always rain in the neighbourhood, we were only visited by it about once in two days. Thunder and lightning were, however, occurring every moment. The sandy soil of this neighbourhood abounds in vitreous concretions, apparently the result of the lightning entering the ground; and a native told me it was not uncommon for houses to be struck by the electric fluid. Notwithstanding such occasional accidents, the periodicity of these storms serves to destroy that sense of fear with which we ourselves are apt to look upon these displays of the power of Nature.

The house I had engaged was a brick-built one, very commodious, and was possessed of a small yard in front, in which I tethered my ass. As I had no one to attend upon me, I had to go every day to market to make my purchases, and on such occasions would lock my door and take the key with me. The door-locks in the East are of a very peculiar description, consisting of a kind of large square wooden bolt on the outside, which is so constructed as to receive on its insertion into the jamb of the door three small iron pegs, which drop into it from above. This bolt is possessed also of a groove, along which, on opening, a

wooden key is run, having three iron pegs fixed in it
corresponding to the others, and by which these latter
are raised, and the bolt thus allowed to be withdrawn.

I had sold my kitchen utensils at Khartoum, out of
respect to the feelings of my donkey, and so now possessed no convenience for the preparation of food, except
a solitary coffee-pot. In these large towns, however,
public "dining-rooms" are not difficult to find, and
cafés are also plentiful. In the early morning I would go
to one of these latter and get a *finjan* of coffee, which
notwithstanding its being *à la Turque*, that is, very thick,
and without sugar and milk, I always enjoyed. This
café noir is at all times very refreshing, and preferable
to every other beverage on the desert journey.

It is customary amongst the Arabs to eat in the
morning a kind of pancake called *fateer*, which is soaked
in liquid butter and eaten, as usual, with the fingers.
Instead of water being used to wash the hands after this
repast, a bowl of sawdust is passed round in which they
are rubbed; it answers the purpose much better. At
noon and sunset the cook-shops are open with their
penny dishes of stewed camel or goat's flesh; but, in a
general way, I preferred milk and bread, both of which
are remarkably cheap here.

I was greatly troubled while at Wad Medineh with a disease common in the Soudan, breaking out in sores on the legs and feet. Even the animals are troubled with it. The slightest scratch would become soon a running sore, which would remain incurable for two or three months, eating a large hole into the flesh. One on my left foot, occasioned simply by a tight shoe, gave me the most excruciating pain, confining me three weeks to my bed. My books were at such times the only consolation I had.

CHAPTER III.

WAD MEDINEH TO MATAMMAH.

Leave Wad Medineh—Ferry over Blue River—Aboo Harras—
Decline of the town—Again in the desert—River Rahhad—A
waste, howling wilderness—Prairies on fire—Thunderstorm—
Water-cure—Hyenas—Arrival at Gedárif—Open-air market—
Coptic hospitality — Attacks of ague — Move on — Incorrigible
nature of my donkey—Rich country—Cotton plantations—Large
doura—Bruce—Ras el Feel—Gallabat—The Tokruris—Matammah—Shûm of the village—River Atbara—Rich flora—Hyena
resurrectionists—Arrival of the French consul.

ABOUT the 1st of October I quitted Wad Medineh for
Aboo Harras, on the opposite banks of the river, a
little below the junction of the waters of the Rahhad
with those of the Blue Nile. I had about five miles of
the river's western bank to traverse before reaching the
ferry, through a tract covered with thick jungle in the
richest luxuriance, and almost impenetrable—the retreat, I was informed, of wild animals. There were
several boats at the ferry, and the noise and bustle attending the shipment of donkeys, cattle, and the animal

man, was beyond description, and when on board we were so jostled together that I stood in great danger of having my toes trodden off. The river, which is here nearly half a mile broad, was very high, being swollen with the rains, and rushed by with tremendous velocity, carrying with it great quantities of driftwood, torn from the trees in its upper course, and occasionally whole trunks might be seen. These are fished out by the natives for firewood.

We had crossed over, not to the town of Aboo Harras, but to its market, which is held about two miles farther north, for the convenience of other villages which there occupy the river's bank. I had, therefore, this distance to go before I reached it, my road lying over a number of sand-hills for the most part void of vegetation, except here and there a thorny acacia, presenting in this respect a curious contrast with the opposite bank, whose wild luxuriance of foliage looked beautiful across the glassy stream. A solitary dôm palm rises up from amidst the houses of the town, and forms a prominent object in approaching it.

Aboo Harras, like Wad Medineh, is in ruins, occupying not half of its former extent which the large mounds of earth round the town indicate to have been con-

siderable. As the crude sun-dried bricks used in the
construction of houses here cannot be employed a second
time for such a purpose, it is the custom, when a house
begins to decay, to build another alongside of it. Hence
it is that these towns present their semi-dilapidated appearance. Another result also is the continued increase
of level from the accumulation of this débris, so that
one can nearly always judge of the age of a town by its
height. Many of the towns of Egypt and Nubia, and such
as Wad Medineh and Aboo Harras in these parts, are
examples of this; Khartoum and Meselemieh, being
comparatively new towns, still retain their low level.

Two gentlemen, Messrs. Hausmann and Eipperle,
whose acquaintance I had made in Cairo, and who had
left that city a little before me with the object of
establishing one of the Apostel's Strasse Missionary
Stations at Aboo Harras, ignorant like myself of its
great decline, were surprised to find it almost uninhabited. So much for the value of most maps of these
countries. Aboo Harras, with perhaps scarcely 3000,
stands out in enormously big letters, while Meselemieh,
with 20,000, is not even marked. Its only importance
now is, that it is the place where caravans leave the
Nile for Gedárif, Taka, and Abyssinia.

I had to stay ten days here, during which I suffered much from general debility. I was scarcely in a fit state, therefore, when I found camels, to proceed, but the desire of continuing my journey induced me to leave. I had a companion in an Arab merchant, and we were afterwards joined by many others on the road; for here travellers band together for the sake of safety, and as a guarantee against robbers. All these districts are occupied by wild Arab tribes, amongst whom the Shukerieh have the pre-eminence. I had a letter to their sheik, Sultan Aboo Sin, as he is called here, which Mustapha Aga of Luxor had given me; but as his residence was much farther to the north, and out of my route, I did not present it. He is said to be a magnificent fellow, more than six feet in height, and with a long snow-white beard. He was one of the last to hold out against the Egyptian invasion, but at length, tired out by an unequal contest, sent in his submission to the Pasha.

At noon the first day we reached the banks of the Rahhad, where we stopped to fill the water-skins. The Rahhad is a mere narrow stream, running between high jungly banks, but quite unnavigable. It has its sources in the mountains of Abyssinia, near to its sister stream the Dender; and they continue in a parallel course to the Blue River, though not uniting their waters, as represented in Bruce's map. Towards night we were met by another caravan, from one of whom my friend the merchant received a letter to the effect that his wife at Gedárif was dead. He did not take the news at all to heart, assuring me that he had a reserve at Meselemieh, as he found this arrangement much more convenient than having to take a wife with him wherever he went.

On leaving the Rahhad we had to traverse six days of desert; and a desert one of the worst in these parts, not so much from the want of water, but from the want of shade for the noon-time rest. I was excessively weak and ill, having scarcely eaten anything for a week, and yet I had not the slightest appetite. Water was all I could take. On one occasion I thought I was near my end, for I was seized with a terrible feeling of heaviness and giddiness in my head. Whether it was the effects of a sun-stroke, or the result of excessive weakness, I cannot say; an hour or two and it had passed away. But the sun was insufferably hot, and in my agony I scarcely knew what to do. When the time for rest came I could scarcely descend from the camel, I was so weak, and then I would throw myself down beneath the mockery of a shade afforded by some stunted bush or long grass, rolling my head in a blanket as some further protection against the rays of fire darting down from the vertical sun. Other Europeans whom I saw afterwards testified of the hardships and sufferings they had endured in this desert, and the heaps of pebbles on the roadside marked the spots where some had succumbed to its horrors.

I had now entered a country much different from that which I had hitherto traversed. Unlike most deserts, the ground consisted of a soft black soil like garden mould, but perfectly incapable of affording sustenance to a single tree, and supporting only a long reedy grass, which sometimes attained the height of a man on horseback. This in many places had been fired, and it was a remarkably fine sight at night to witness tracts of country of miles in extent of a perfect blaze, which the most copious rains would scarcely serve to extinguish.

The fourth evening we were overtaken by a fearful storm, which lasted all night. The heavy torrents of rain were accompanied by flashes of lightning, immediately succeeded by terrific peals of thunder, showing

D

that we were in the very centre of the electric discharge. The lightning would sometimes flash a few feet from the ground, and in the very midst of our company. In these hot climates the amount of electricity in the atmosphere is immense; I have sometimes seen as many as fifty flashes in a minute. All my things were soaked, and as I soon lost my shoes in the mud, a great part of the night I was ankle-deep in water, as well as not having a dry thread about me. With all this, however, I did not feel cold, and after it was over seemed to feel much better. Hydropathists might be justified in calling it a water-cure.

The following day we reached Jebel Atash, or Thirsty Mountain, and stayed for the night at its foot. Here it was discovered that one of the donkeys of the company had decamped with a load of cotton goods on its back, and a party of three or four immediately returned to look for it. In the meanwhile I lay down to rest, but hereupon was told I must not sleep that night on account of the hyenas which infest the neighbourhood; but as I had had no rest the night before, I did not see the merit of allowing myself to be robbed of it the second time, especially as we had adopted the precaution of discharging a round from our guns as a slight hint to any wild beasts in the vicinity of our being prepared to give them a warm reception should they molest us. About three hours after, the party who had gone in search of the lost donkey returned, but without the beast. No doubt the poor animal fell a prey to the "laughable" hyenas, as Mrs. Brown would have it. Another day and a half and we arrived at Gedárif, our destination.

Gedárif, a little south of the ancient Mandera, and 100 miles south-east of the Blue River, is situated at the foot of some low hills which form the prelude to the high mountainous country of Abyssinia. It consists of a number of scattered villages, the principal called Hellet es-Sook, or the market town. This is held twice a week, and is exceedingly well supplied. These open-air markets, a great number of which I have seen during my wanderings, are a very interesting sight to a stranger. One part is devoted to the sale of camels, cattle, sheep, and goats; another to that of corn and doura; another, milk and butter; another, raw cotton, dates, &c. The butcher slaughters his meat on the spot, whether ox, sheep, or camel. The camel is killed somewhat differently from the rest; for it may well be imagined that a camel with merely its throat cut might be a long while in dying. They therefore adopt the mode of striking it with a long knife at once to the heart, having previously taken care to tie his long legs in a manner that he cannot move. The rest of the market is occupied by the stalls of the linendraper—if so he may be called—who, as is not uncommon with us in country towns, is grocer as well. Salt is also a staple commodity in the Gedárif market, being brought from the coasts of the Red Sea, by way of Souakim and Kassala, and hence transported to Matammah and North Abyssinia. Much coffee and sesame pass through here on the way to Souakim.

Gedárif is on the high-road which connects North Abyssinia and the countries on the Blue River with the Red Sea at Souakim, and so with Egypt and Arabia. It is very much frequented by merchants and *hajjis* (pilgrims), and on the whole is considered pretty safe. One case of murder, however, happened a short time before my arrival—that of a Greek trader. It was alleged that he had been killed by a lion, but the evidence to the contrary was too great to admit of the supposition.

The house of a Copt named Maalim Georgis is generally open for the accommodation of European travellers, and there consequently I went. I was kindly received and welcomed until I should have occasion to go forward. This I am sorry to say I was unable to do for a fortnight, for I had no sooner arrived in the house than I was seized with a fit of ague, which continued daily for more than a week; and how much longer it might have lasted I cannot say, for then a young Greek gave me a dose of quinine, which happily put a stop to it. It generally came on about 2 P.M., the ague lasting about an hour, being succeeded by three hours' fever, and ending in a profuse perspiration. It rendered me excessively weak, so that I could not even sit up, but was obliged to keep my bed all day. I was also troubled with what I took to be the effects of a sunstroke, but it may have simply been the result of the weak state I was in. One day when I went to the market to see about hiring a camel, I felt a sudden blindness, a film coming over my eyes which prevented me from distinguishing objects at half a yard's distance. This lasted for more than an hour, during which time I wandered about groping for the house, and till the dimness had passed away I was utterly unable to find it, though it was only fifty yards off.

Having at last succeeded in engaging a camel, I left Gedárif for Matammah, four days' journey to the south.

We started at midnight, as the camel-driver seemed in a great hurry to get forward. These people are very fantastic and arbitrary in their way of travelling, sometimes hurrying you on both night and day for no earthly reason except their own caprice, at others stopping two or three days at a place merely for the sake of visiting friends or of a booza-drinking. I got so vexed at last by this irregular manner of proceeding that I thought it high time to have a will of my own, and when they used to come to shake me up at 2 or 3 o'clock in the morning I told them I would not budge till daylight. My weak condition made these irregularities the worse to bear.

Two hours before daybreak we stopped at a place to fill the girbas with water, and while thus engaged my dreadful donkey, which was still with me, though pensioned off as it were, took it into his head to go and reconnoitre a little. He cost us a delay of three hours, so that our night's travelling in the end availed us very little. He was caught about a mile off taking an early breakfast by himself, perfectly regardless of the anxiety we had suffered on his account.

The appearance of the country was now beautiful. The farther we advanced the hills became higher and higher, clothed to their summits with foliage in every variety of green. The rains had quite renewed the face of the earth. The lowlands were richly cultivated, abounding in plantations of cotton, sesame, and doura ; and here, if anywhere, extensive cotton growing may be tried to the best advantage. Any amount of land may be had for nothing, and when it has been cleared of the thorny trees and long grass, it is in every way adapted to the growth of the plant. Some of the plantations I passed were very extensive, and perfectly white with the cotton. The simplest way of clearing the land is by means of fire. The long reedy grass is so thick and strong that a person might lean his back against it without its giving way, and it is quite impenetrable to either man or animals. The trees are also very numerous, and, even when the fire has done its work, much labour is required in extirpating the roots. There are two great objections, however, to a European settling here—the first being the insalubrity of the climate, the second the difficulty in obtaining free labour. The German missionaries at Matammah received a sum of money from a Manchester firm to induce them to try cotton-growing, but I have not heard of their having succeeded.

Midway between Gedárif and Matammah is Doka, a large village surrounded by vast doura plantations. The doura of this district was the finest I had seen, rising frequently to a height of ten or twelve feet, and possessing ears or spikes of corn a foot long, and a pound or more in weight. In reaping, the ears only are cut off; the stalks are left standing to serve as fodder for the cattle, the strongest being used in the construction of houses. A bunch of doura is not unfrequently found suspended from the roofs of the houses as a specimen of the last crop, or perhaps as a charm to ensure a favourable one the ensuing season. The young green stalks are sometimes chewed by the people as a substitute for sugar-cane. I had to stay at Doka two days to please the camel-driver, who objected to go forward until companions for the road were found, alleging that the country was dangerous to persons travelling alone.

I was now on the road traversed by Bruce, and the district I was passing through formed in his time the Abyssinian province of Ras el Feel, and the government of it was conferred by the king upon the British traveller himself. It is in the possession of the Tokruris, negro immigrants from Central Africa. They mostly have come from Darfour and Dar Selay, and their original object appears to have been simply the pilgrimage to Mecca; but finding on their way to the Holy City this fruitful country almost uninhabited, on their return they settled here, first in small numbers, then in greater, until the country, some hundred miles in extent, fell into their possession. But they had not settled long in this district before they excited the animosity of the Abyssinians on one side and the Turks on the other, and it is only on condition of a tribute paid severally to Abyssinians and Turks that they are suffered to remain. The province now passes by the name of Gellabat, and the seat of government, vested in the hands of a sheik or *shûm*, as he is here called, is at Matammah. Here I arrived the sixth day from Gedárif.

I went at once to the house of my German friend, Mr. Hausmann, who, with his companion, had resolved to establish a Missionary station here, after relinquishing their ideas of Aboo Harras. There is no doubt but that Matammah possesses immense advantages over Aboo Harras for this purpose, for it is better populated; the people, though Moslems, are more susceptible to Christian instruction, and here the languages of that part of the Soudan between Lake Tchad and Kordofan may be acquired preparatory to extended labour in those countries. Its greatest drawback is the unhealthiness of the climate; but even this is somewhat compensated for by the vicinity of the mountains of Abyssinia, which form an excellent sanatorium in case of sickness.

Though the name of Matammah, or even that of Gellabat, does not appear in Bruce, it may be identified with his Hor Cacamoot, the Valley of the Shadow of Death, the name of which is no great promise of the agreeableness of the place. In appearance, however, it is very far from being disagreeable, situated as it is in a wide fertile valley, through which courses a small stream on its way to connect itself with the Atbara, a few miles distant. The town possesses perhaps 500 huts, the largest occupied by the shûm, a good-natured negro, who is the acknowledged head of the Tokruri colonists. He is a very active man, always superintending in person any building, clearing of ground, and such like improvements taking place in the village, and on one occasion I saw him with a besom sweeping up rubbish around his own hut. He is not without a certain kind of dignity, however; and when he holds his levée has a number of soldiers with drawn swords and muskets around his divan. The time when he is willing to give a hearing to complaints or to receive visitors is always signified by the loud beat of kettle-drums. Whenever he goes out he always has a fore-runner, called the shûm's mouthpiece, who bellows out in a most horrid yell his intimation of the great man's approach.

Matammah is an important place, on account of its situation on the high-road to Abyssinia and its being the last place on the frontier. It has a great market for cotton, horses, mules, and cattle. Cotton is supplied to Abyssinia, being the growth of the district between Gedárif and Matammah; the live stock is brought down from the former country. A few slaves are sold here, being kept in private houses, where the purchases are transacted.

Four miles from Matammah the banks of the Atbara are reached, which is here a broad rapid stream, passing through a country rich in its flora, possessing amongst other trees the baobab, sycamore, and a kind of cedar. Its banks abound with every variety of wild beast—the elephant, lion, rhinoceros, and hyena. Gazelles, ante-lopes, and giraffes are also found. The hyena is everywhere about here as common as dogs with us; hundreds of them are prowling about the houses at night. While lying in bed I could often hear them snuffing on the outside for some bone or refuse that might have been thrown out during the day. As the people do not dig deep graves here, it is not uncommon to see many of these emptied of their contents by hyena resurrectionists. They are cowardly animals, and seldom attack men; but I was told of two cases at Matammah —one of a maniac who was wandering out at night, and who was killed and eaten; the other that of a woman, but she was only bitten.

The kind reception given me by Messrs. Hausmann and Eipperle induced me to prolong my stay, and while here M. Lejean, the French consul, on his way to his post in Abyssinia, arrived. We of course agreed to go together, or rather, I should say, he kindly allowed me to accompany him. M. Lejean is well known in the geographical world by his topographical researches in the Danubian principalities, but more so by his having been entrusted with an expedition to discover the sources of the Nile, which, notwithstanding its having failed, has furnished us with much information relative to the western branches of the White River, and the interesting tribes which occupy those countries. In accepting the Abyssinian consulate, M. Lejean had an eye to exploration and research in this interesting country, and, as will be seen, he afterwards had good opportunity for accomplishing his object.

CHAPTER IV.

Enter Abyssinia—Ill-defined frontier—The Switzerland of Africa—
Earthly paradise—Slight adventure—River Coang—Wekhni—
Abyssinian exclusiveness—Detention at Wekhni—Magnificent
view—Teff—Again on the march—An European a *rara avis*—
Custom-house authority—Abyssinian inhospitality—*In nubibus*—
Cool climate—View of Lake Tsana—Enter Tchelga—Impudence
of natives—Muscular Christianity.

In the afternoon of November 24, 1862, in company
with M. Lejean, the French consul, I left Matammah
in the country of the Tokruris for Abyssinia. The
frontier is very indefinitely marked; but as for four
days the country is almost uninhabited, there is no great
necessity for an exact line of division. The River Coang,
situated midway between Matammah and Wekhni, the
first village of Abyssinia, is the most natural boundary.
The possibility is, that King Theodore still lays claim
to the Tokruri country as being properly a part of
Abyssinia, and an Abyssinian sovereign has perhaps

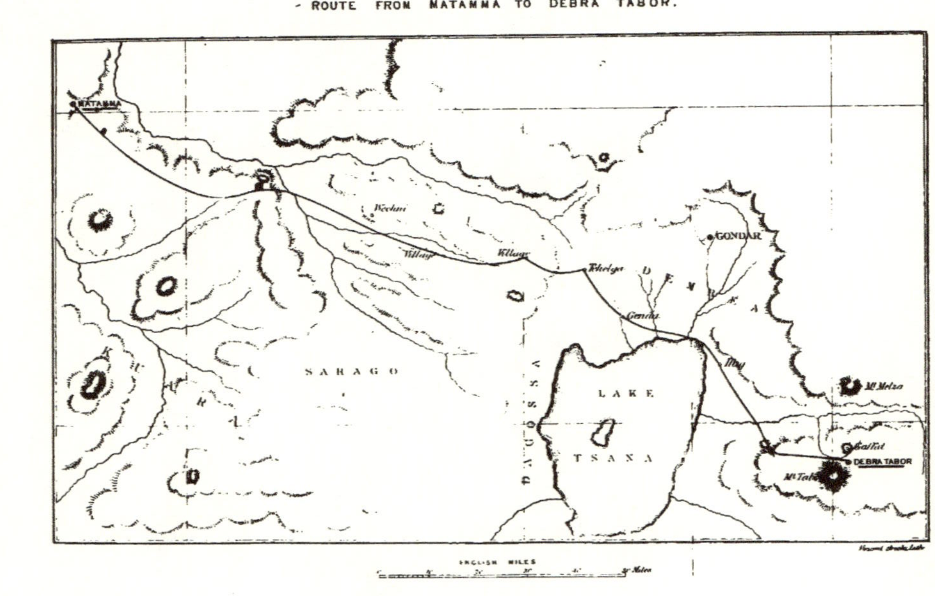
ROUTE FROM MATAMMA TO DEBRA TABOR.
MATAMMA
GONDAR
DEMBEA
Wochni
Village
Village
Tchelga
Gendra
SARAGO
DAGOSSA
LAKE
TSANA
Ifag
Mt Melza
Saifat
DEBRA TABOR
Mt Tabor
ENGLISH MILES
Vincent Brooks, Lith.

a greater right to it than a Turk, but the tribute-money
and dread of Egyptian arms has hitherto restrained
Theodore's attempt to exercise his claim.

The road was very uneven, now ascending a steep
mountain-side, now descending into a deep valley. The
country was magnificent, far surpassing anything I had
previously seen. The high mountains of the Scotch
highlands, covered with the fertility of the Rhine-land,
would best represent it; but the vegetation was of a
nature quite different from that of the Rhine, characterised as it was by the luxuriance of the tropics. Once
the road skirted the side of a mountain the summit
of which, raised 1000 feet above our heads, looked
down into a deep valley another thousand below our
feet. On the opposite side of the valley the land
rose to a similarly steep eminence, which, in one part,
was connected to that on which we stood by a low chain
of undulating ground, so that a pretty little stream at
the bottom, like a silver thread in the dark shadow of
the mountains, wound about searching for its channel.
Fruitful fields hung over it thick at every curve. The
hills, of secondary formation, were broken here and there
into rocky chasms, through which leaped innumerable
falls of water in their downward course to join the

stream ; and here I saw for the first time the beautiful
Euphorbia called the Kolquol, whose dark candelabra-
shaped branches, tipped with bright yellow flowers,
stood out in deep relief from the lighter green around.
Bright flowers of every variety, most of which were
unknown to me, but amongst others the familiar wild-
rose, the honeysuckle, and jessamine, lent their beauty
and fragrance to the scene. The whole was a perfect
gem of Nature.

On one occasion we had a small adventure. We
were resting one night near the summit of a mountain,
when about two hours before daybreak we were awaked
by a loud hubbub and the discharge of a gun. Start-
ing to our feet, we inquired what was up, and our
anxiety was increased by M. Lejean's Arab seizing the
second gun and discharging it. All I saw, for it was
pitch dark, was one of the mules kicking about amongst
the ashes of a half-extinguished fire, and endeavouring
to extricate himself from the leather thong which bound
his head to a tree. This he soon succeeded in doing,
and went off at a furious rate towards the woods which
clothe the sides of the mountain. I thought he had
burnt himself at the fire, and that this was the cause
of his breaking loose, but the rest maintained that he

had been bitten by the hyenas: and they were right, for at daybreak we saw and gave chase to one of these brutes, who was still prowling about. He was only a short distance off, but not being certain of my skill as a marksman, I tried to get nearer before I shot at him. The animal was too wary, and, though in his flight he frequently turned round to have a look at us, he was careful to keep at a safe distance. These creatures were much bolder here than near the villages, and would sometimes, as in the present instance, come across our path, even in daylight. I found in this spot traces of the rhinoceros. As we were sleeping in the open air, with our faces exposed, it was fortunate for us that the hyenas preferred trying mule's flesh to man's. We heard afterwards that the mule had returned to Matammah, a distance of forty miles, but was so severely bitten in the flank that he was perfectly useless.

The River Coang was swollen with the rains, and my donkey required much manual persuasion to be induced to cross, and then he refused to take me over, but obliged me to wade. During the whole of the journey he was a mortification to me; for having been born and bred on the flats of Khartoum, he could not or would not accommodate himself to the roughness of the roads.

On the fifth day we arrived at Wekhni, the first village in Abyssinia, where is held a large market. All merchandise is here transferred from the camel to the mule and donkey, as the former useful animal is incapable of traversing the rugged roads by which this mountainous country is entered. The market is held on a narrow plain, studded here and there with thick shady trees, amongst the boughs of which are great numbers of paroquets and other gay-plumaged birds. Beneath one of these, in the dry bed of a mountain-torrent, we encamped, determined to rest that day, and proceed on to Tchelga on the morrow. Thanks to Abyssinian jealousy and suspicion, no such luck was in store for us. Here we had to undergo an examination worse than that to which one used to be subjected on Austrian frontiers. The same afternoon we were visited by the shûm, who, having been informed that M. Lejean was the French consul proceeding with presents to their king, nevertheless refused him permission to pass until he should give him a *bachsheesh*. The demand having been almost anticipated, the consul was not loth to comply with it, and we settled down for the night with the intention of proceeding at sunrise. The following morning, however, the treacherous old sinner, notwithstanding that he had received his present, declared that without the permission of Balambaras Guelmo of Tchelga we could not proceed, and that we must remain there until a messenger had been despatched to that functionary for a permit. Our arms were then seized, and we were bundled off up a steep mountain-side, on whose summit, 1000 feet above the market-place, were a few rude huts, in one of which we were to be accommodated during the five days of the messenger's absence. Of course nothing was furnished us, and we had to pay exorbitantly for the little food we purchased.

The ignorance and impudence of the people were great, they not being able to distinguish Europeans from Turks, and insulting us on the supposition that we were the latter. M. Lejean, who was a topographer and geologist, of course went about to inspect the country and collect specimens. They interpreted his proceedings as a survey of their land with the intention of taking it. "What should he go scouring the country round for?" said one of them, knowingly, "in search of stones, when there are plenty at his house-door, and much bigger?" While taking a walk once in the neighbourhood, a woman hooted us at the top of her voice until we got out of hearing, our only offence having been the plucking of a few wild flowers.

The view from the summit of Wekhni mountain is very fine, embracing an extent of thirty miles on each side. This part of the country consists of vast table-lands of transition rock, intercepted by deep valleys of undulating ground, partly cultivated, but for the most part covered with wood. The flat summits of the higher lands are entirely bare. We saw here, for the first time, the grain called *teff*, consisting of what at first would be taken for long grass run to seed. It stands about a foot high, and yields a small round grain not larger than a pin's head. It makes good sweet bread, however, which is much preferred by the natives to that of the *mashila* (doura or maize), or even to wheaten bread.

The messenger at length returned, and we were told that we could proceed, and at the same time our arms were restored to us. We were also furnished with an Amhara guide, whom the consul agreed to reward at the journey's end. On reaching the foot of the moun-tain we met a German baron of the name of Dablin, who had come to Abyssinia with Captain Cameron, the

British consul, by way of Massowah, and was now leaving for Khartoum. He heartily cursed the people, at which we did not marvel from the little we had seen of them. He uttered a truth which might serve as a caution to every traveller who enters the country. "Abyssinia is a place to teach patience to a man who has it not, and take it away from him who has." An European is such a *rara avis* in these parts that we were induced to stay the rest of the day in the baron's company, exchanging a few notes of our respective journeys. Having a guide from the king with him, he thought he was going to pass the frontier more easily than we had done; but in this he was mistaken, as we afterwards heard, for the Wekhnians not only took his firearms, but, on his leaving, refused to restore them, and, though he wrote to the king about the matter, I do not think he even received them in the end.

Our troubles had only commenced at Wekhni, for the same day we left we were stopped on the road by a man who chose to call himself the custom-house keeper, and who had the audacity to seize our arms again. He had already got the consul's, and, coming to where I was, laid his hand on mine, but in a moment I seized it from him, and stood prepared to contest it, should he

persist. He saw I was determined, and so gave th
matter up. He demanded ten dollars duty on the three
donkey-loads of M. Lejean, although we told him that
they consisted of gifts for the king himself. This did
not avail, but he at last took five dollars. What vexed
us most was that the young man who had been sent
with us as guide, though he knew we had got proper
permission to pass, encouraged rather than prevented
this attempt to detain us.

The succeeding evening we had experience of Abyssinian hospitality. We had hitherto been traversing
a long valley through a forest of tall bamboos, but
towards dusk we ascended on to an extensive plateau,
on the summit of which we found a large village. It
had been raining during the day, and the ground
was wet, so we asked in the name of the French
consul, on a visit to Theodore, for a hut to sleep in.
This was positively refused; and as it soon recommenced raining, we were soaked through, and had to
pass the night in that pleasant state, with the houses
only a dozen yards off. Well might Ahmed the Arab
say that he had never seen such people before, though
he had traversed the country from Alexandria to the
White River, and we could not wonder at his uttering

a fervent *Allah yektaahum,* "May God cut them off."
And these were Christians, who knew that we also were
Christians! Really I had for the moment a sensation
of shame in thinking of the liberal, unfailing hospitality
of the Moslem.

We were now some 7000 feet above the sea-level,
and the air was very cool. Sometimes even we were en-
veloped in clouds, and though the real wet season was
over, showers were still frequent. After traversing the
high plateau for a distance of about five miles, we began
to descend gradually towards the plain in which Tchelga
is situated, and in this descent we caught the first view
of the calm waters of Lake Tsana. The nearer shores
were plainly discernible, as well as the wooded islands
which stud its northern surface. Its more remote out-
line, however, was lost in the dim distance; but the
upper peaks of the mountains of Gojam were visible
beyond. The first view of this noted water-supply of
the Blue River, so long reckoned as the real Nile, filled
my mind with new and strange emotions. The whole
district seemed sanctified with the remembrance of the
indefatigable Bruce.

An hour or two afterwards we reached the village of
Tchelga. As Tchelga is the capital of the district, we

thought that here at least we should be accommodated with a house. Far from that, we were led to the centre of the plain, and the goods unloaded beneath a small mimosa tree, which was a mockery of a shade from the noontide heat. I asked to be led to the shade of some thick kolquol trees a short distance off. This they refused, so we were obliged patiently to submit. The last alternative was not rendered the more easy by the thick clouds which soon came rolling towards us from the east. The approaching storm formed another and stronger reason for some indoor accommodation, but the people, who gathered round to grin at us, quietly walked away when they saw the rain coming on, leaving us to protect ourselves from the wet as best we could. We of course made for the nearest hut, which proved to be a donkey stable. M. Lejean then sent his Arab to engage a house for money, and he returned and said there were two to be had, one for ourselves and the other for the animals. The one for us proved to be the identical donkey stable we had taken shelter in—a miserable place, not more than six feet square, and so badly roofed that it continued raining inside long after the exterior rain had ceased. However, the consul agreed, and ordered Ahmed to remove the baggage out of the wet. While he was proceeding to do this, the man who had acted as guide sat watching him; but no sooner had he loaded one mule and was moving towards the hut, than the Abyssinian jumped up and caught hold of the bridle, saying we must stay outside until we had seen the shûm—as if a French consul was to sit in the rain until that official thought good to give him a reception! I saw the man's movements from a distance, so rushing out of the house across the plain, I scarcely gave him time to reply to my "Let go!" before I struck him on the mouth with my fist in a way that made him let go quicker than words would have done. He made an ignominious retreat. His call for assistance, however, soon attracted the whole neighbourhood, and in the midst of the excitement I saw the people coming from all quarters, as it might have been to a Scotch gathering. Thinking the first who came to interfere was about to strike me, I did not wait for his blow, but struck out—not, however, effectually. He closed, and by his superior strength sent me "to grass" in a moment. He was now on top, and being a powerful fellow, much more than a match for myself, already reduced by continued fever (the last at Wekhni), I might soon have become thoroughly *hors de combat* had not the rest interfered and liberated me. This incident was the signal for a council, in which it was discussed what to do with these troublesome Franjis, and, after a good deal of squabbling, it was resolved that if we would deliver up our arms to the *nagadaras* or *shûm* we should be furnished with a hut. We agreed, and so they conducted us through a grove of kolquols to one on the side of a neighbouring hill. It is probable that our show of vigour and subsequent submission gained this for us.

CHAPTER V.

TCHELGA TO GAFFAT.

Detention at Tchelga—Bad accommodation—Tchelga and its market
—Salt currency—Semi-incarceration—Neighbourhood of Tchelga
—Iron and coal—Kolquol trees—Native clothing—Queer law-
suits—Get impatient—Visit to Balambaras Guelmo—Beautiful
country — Moslem village — The Guimb — Mountain fastness—
Presentation to the chief—Our suit granted—A Christmas dinner
—Return to Tchelga—Depart for Genda—Mr. Flad and the
Falashas—Adopt the native costume—En route for Debra Tabor
—Lake Tsana—Plains in rich cultivation—A truant spirit—
Mount Tabor.

" GOOD accommodation for man or beast " is sought for
in vain in Abyssinia. We had to endure horrible inconvenience in the wretched hovel which had been
assigned to us as our residence during the interval
which should elapse until the return of the messenger
who had been despatched to inform his majesty of the
French consul's arrival. We occupied an ill-thatched
circular hut, of some eight yards in diameter, the
biggest half of which was occupied by the two mules

and the donkeys, leaving very inadequate bed-space for the two-legged animals who were doomed to seek (not find) proper accommodation therein. The latter should have included only the consul, myself, and the Arab; but the impudence of the natives induced many of them to seek a retreat in our hut for the night, until, articles having been stolen, we asserted our rights by blocking up the doorway. This did not exclude some other intruders, in the shape of goats, dogs, and fowls, who made their way through the interstices of the reed enclosure which formed the wall of the hut, and which also gave abundant entrance to the cold night air of these mountain districts. These vexations, coupled with the unpleasantness of being occasionally trodden on by the fidgety beasts, and bitten by the innumerable fleas and bugs with which all Abyssinian houses abound, formed the uncomfortable adjuncts of a three weeks' residence in the miserable village of Tchelga.

Tchelga is the name given to the province north of Dembea, but it is also applied to the village claiming to be its capital. This right is supported by the fact of its possessing an occasional market, where the more immediate wants of the neighbourhood are supplied. It is held in the open plain, where the articles

r sale are spread out on the surface of the ground;
 booth of any kind for such a purpose is an un-
nown convenience in Abyssinia.   During our visit the
1arket was said to be not so well supplied as usual,
he king's soldiers being then billeted in the neigh-
ourhood, who have a great licence in robbery of cattle,
1ules, and articles of food.   Raw cotton and coarse
loth, tanned hides, honey, grain, milk, butter, red
epper, coffee, *tshat* (a sort of tea), *kosso*, and sweet
otatoes, were the principal articles I saw.   The Maria
'heresa dollar is the only coin used in these transac-
.ons under the name of *bir* (silver).   This piece must
e of a certain kind, however, containing the spots
·hich form the queen's tiara, and other marks clearly
efined; for which reason it is called by the Arabs of
1e Soudan, Abou Nukter, or father of spots.   Of course
1e dollar can be used only in large purchases, and
; quite inadequate for ordinary market transactions.
maller purchases are therefore made with pieces of
1lt called *tsho*, which are the monetary medium
hroughout the greater part of Abyssinia.   This salt
; obtained from extensive mines in the country of the
)anakil, where it is cut into small blocks, eight inches
)ng by one inch and a half in breadth, each of which

is of a variable market value of between 2*d*. and 3*d*. In some districts, where dollars are scarce, the transport of salt to market implies the necessity of a porter.

The time spent at Tchelga was occupied in taking daily excursions in the neighbourhood, notwithstanding that thereby we incurred the displeasure of the people. Perhaps they took us for spies in the service of the Turks, who were then expected to be about to make a threatening descent on their northern frontiers. On one occasion the consul, having wandered alone some considerable distance from the village, was seized and taken to a house where he was to be detained until further particulars could be ascertained of the intentions of this strange visitor; but their vigilance having abated a little after an hour or two, M. Lejean took to his heels, and managed to reach the village again without further molestation. I was greatly relieved by the sight of him. Henceforth, therefore, we had to moderate our excursions within more narrow limits.

Through the undulating plains of Tchelga run several small streams, which drain the waters of the higher lands into the River Angueab on the north, and others

vhich take their course in an opposite direction to
ᴊake Tsana. This double watershed seemed to occa-
ion M. Lejean no little difficulty in his topographical
ketches of the neighbourhood, which was somewhat
ncreased by the ferruginous nature of the rocks destroy-
ng the determinative power of his delicate compass,
ometimes, when placed on the ground, to a matter of
)0°. The presence of iron was further evidenced by
he slimy yellow deposits of oxide which some of the
nountain rivulets make in their course. Beds of an
nferior coal we also found in the plain of Tchelga, laid
ᴊare by a small stream which had dug for itself a pas-
ᴊage of some forty feet deep. The fact of the presence
ᴊf coal, not only here but also in many other parts of
Abyssinia, seems to point to sources of wealth possessed
by this country, which only an enlightened Government is required to open out. What an inestimable
advantage it would be if Aden could be supplied with
this valuable mineral from Abyssinia instead of round
the Cape.*

* I observe from a letter of Mr. Hausmann's, published in
" Christian Work " of May, 1864, that the neighbourhood of Tchelga
has since my visit been worked, and 150 loads (mule or horse, certainly not cart, as the latter does not exist in the country)
despatched to the German workmen at Gaffat.

On the summit of the hill on which our hut was situated may be found traces of the ruins of a square stone building, which perhaps formed originally a Portuguese church, but which has yielded to a more modern structure of wattle and dab, where the present inhabitants of Tchelga perform their devotions. As usual in buildings of such a description, this is situated in the midst of a beautiful grove of trees, amongst which the kolquol, by its beauty, claims an undisputed preference. It here attains a height of forty feet, and the cactus-like branches, springing from the parent-stem about ten feet from the ground, are some six inches in thickness, and yield on contusion a bitter milky fluid which is said to be poisonous. The wild aloe, about two feet high, and adorned with a beautiful red flower, is also very common in this neighbourhood. The plain in which Tchelga is situated is under extensive cultivation, surpassing anything I had seen since leaving Egypt; but nevertheless the people appear to be very poor, living in conical huts of the most wretched description, and many clothed in nothing but sheep-skins, which are thrown over one shoulder and fastened at the opposite hip, and reach a little below the knee. These people are not inexpert in the tanning of hides,

ie face of which they are in the habit of dyeing red.
hree large hides thus finished will sell for a dollar,
) that many clothe themselves in leather. Once in
'chelga I saw a beggarman going about stark naked.

The nagadaras or shûm of the village lived in the
ouse adjoining our own, and as he is " borough magis-
ate," we often had occasion to witness lawsuits be-
ween individuals of this litigious community. The
agadaras is subject to be called out any time, either
y day or night, to settle these differences. He is
n such occasions generally attended by a conclave of
reybeards, who seem to act as a kind of jury; and
hile they are seated on the ground, the plaintiff,
efendant, and witnesses stand in front, always with
houlders bared. The oath administered on these
ccasions, and forming a frequent asseveration through-
ut the whole of the case, is that of *Teodoros yemoot*,
May Theodore (the king) die!" *i. e.* if I speak not
ruth. The Abyssinians differ from the Arabs in this
espect, swearing always by the death of a person rather
han by the life. The plaintiff is then allowed to urge
is complaint, during which time not a word is to be
ttered by any party present, and at the end he seizes
is adversary's and even the judge's *shamaa* (cotton

F

cloth) and makes a large knot in the corner. The defendant is then allowed to make his reply, and he, at the conclusion, ties a corresponding knot in the *shamaa* of the plaintiff or judge. During the course of the suit the knots get fastened and unfastened, though from ignorance of the language I was at a loss to know the whys and the wherefores. The eloquence with which each party urges his cause, and the comparative order in which the whole is conducted—so different from the hubbub in which affairs of this kind are conducted amongst the Arabs—are very remarkable.

Most of the cases which come before these petty judges are not difficult of settlement, but occasionally they have to decide questions which would tax the wisdom of Solomon. I heard of the case of a woman who had a child which was claimed by three fathers, and she herself could not help the judge out of his difficulty.

After a fortnight spent in a kind of semi-incarceration we began to feel in good earnest the monotony of our unpleasant position. At the consul's request, therefore, I wrote a letter to Balambaras Guelmo, governor of the province, who resides about fifteen miles to the north of the village, stating the nature of

M. Lejean's visit, and our desire of continuing the journey. This was despatched by a native, who bore also a present for the governor. Somewhat to my surprise, I must confess, my dog-Arabic was understood by some one in waiting on the Balambaras, and a soldier was despatched to inform us that we should still have to wait the return of the messenger sent to the king, but in the meanwhile the nagadaras was charged to attend a little more to our comfort. The soldier had another duty to perform in the name of his master— to make an examination of the presents brought by M. Lejean for his Abyssinian Majesty. Of course the report of what was going on brought all the neighbours into the hut, and the consul had the mortification of seeing beautiful silks, cloths, &c., subjected to the investigating touch of greasy hands in all directions. During our further stay he was continually pestered by people begging for some of the rich things they had seen.

In the meantime Mr. Flad, the now well-known missionary of the London Society for Promoting Christianity amongst the Jews, residing at Genda, twenty miles to the south, heard how we were situated, and wrote on our behalf to Guelmo to induce him to allow us to go forward to that place and wait there until the king had been acquainted of our arrival. At the same time Mr. Flad wrote to us to inform us of what he had done, and we now thought it advisable to seek an interview with the governor himself to urge our suit.

Having made the resolve, and received permission from the nagadaras, we set out one afternoon. The district we had to pass through was very beautiful—the frequent rains serving to clothe the country with the richest luxuriance. Nature here appears always to put on a splendid robe, like a beautiful woman richly scented ; for here the wild rose is more common than with us, and jessamine, honeysuckle, and other flowers abound : the number and variety of them covering the bushes and the trees gave a gorgeous colouring to the landscape, that few artists would dare to put on canvas, for fear of seeming to overstep the bounds of truth.

The same evening we arrived at a village of Moslem Abyssinians, where the solid appearance of the houses, in many of which cotton-cloth manufacture was going on, but more especially the free hospitality at once granted us, contrasted strongly with the exclusiveness and unthriftiness of the Christian villages we had already seen. Our feet having been washed by females in attendance, we were presented with a supper of teff bread and *shimbra* (peas-pudding)—in which latter, however, Cayenne pepper so predominated that we were necessitated to confine ourselves to bread and a little milk, which was also kindly furnished us. Our beasts also were well foddered. In good humour at this exceptional kind treatment, which the consul did not leave unrewarded, we continued our journey on the morrow.

Our road now stretched over the length of a valley, but gradually ascended until we reached the summit of the mountain on which the governor resides, and from which he takes his name of Bal-amba-ras, this signifying the "master of the mountain-top." This mountain, 8000 feet above the sea, has an offshoot on its eastern side, which is separated from the main body by a chasm of 1000 feet in depth, the only connecting link being a mound of earth and débris, partly artificial, by which a passage is effected on to its summit. This vast rock, as it may be called, possesses a surface of about half a mile square, perfectly flat, and equal in height to the neighbouring plateau. Its four sides are quite perpendicular, so that one leap from the top would hurl you a thousand feet into the valley below. The view from the summit is magnificent in the extreme, surpassing beyond expression anything I have seen. Each direction embraces an extent of nearly fifty miles, the horizon comprising high fantastic peaks, whose summits touch the very skies, and vast plateaus, whose sides, like that on which we stood, fell abruptly to depths exceeding 1000 feet. The valleys below re-sembled, from their undulating surface, a vast sea, whose bright green waves washed the rocky feet of each mountain giant. As may be imagined, the Guimb (tower), for such the rock is named, is an admirable natural fortress, its value being enhanced by its pos-sessing, in a cleft accessible from the top, a constant fountain of water; and there is no doubt but that in the troubled state of Abyssinia Guelmo had chosen it with such a view as his residence.

Balambaras Guelmo is one of the principal chiefs of Abyssinia, and one of a council of five who at the com-mencement of Theodore's reign swore eternal allegiance and unlimited obedience to their king. He is intrusted with the care of some of his Majesty's state prisoners, great warriors, and men of noble family, who by their liberty would endanger the stability of Theodore's throne. These are imprisoned on a neighbouring moun-tain, bound in silver chains, whose length allows them the privilege of taking a stroll round about their houses. Guelmo is governor of the district or province of Tchelga, one of the most fruitful in Abyssinia.

We were detained two hours before we could obtain an interview. We were then ushered into a dark room, whose obscurity at first prevented us from seeing anything. We had no difficulty, however, in hearing a voice, which shouted out in a most jovial tone, *Tyïbin?* *Tyïbin?* the Arabic for "How do you do? Are you well?" We replied to each salutation by a low bow, at the same time assuring the unseen one of our good health, and inquiring how the voice did. The shroud of darkness in which we did *not* behold the chief is here considered to add to the importance of the great man, that vulgar eyes may not gaze too plainly upon his glory. It is an Eastern idea, probably alluded to by St. Paul when he says, "Now we gaze through a glass darkly, but then face to face." Before proceeding to business we were well supplied with *tedge* or honey-wine, which was followed by the strong arracky of the country, neat; so that before the interview was over we, who had not touched strong waters for a long period, were slightly affected by them. We should assuredly have refused to drink, especially the arracky, but we were afraid of giving offence. Our request to visit Mr. Flad was freely granted, for which we tendered our thanks, and gave him a little "soft solder" —at least I interpreted the consul's speech to that effect. The consul presented to him some boxes of powder and percussion-caps, but he was greedy enough to send afterwards for a gun.

As it was too late to return that day, we passed the night on the Guimb, a house and food being supplied us at the governor's order. The latter consisted of a sheep, teff bread, and some more wine. Of the wine we had had quite enough, so we gave it to the servants. The mutton, on the other hand, was covered so thick with red pepper that we could not touch it. The fondness these people have for hot condiments is really amazing. Not only do they use pepper to meats, but it is mixed in their bread, in milk, and even in the water they drink. It is here called Berberee, probably from the Berber country to the north, where much is grown. On after occasions I managed to eat the hot dishes pretty well, but before my mouth had grown accustomed to it they were intolerable to me. What made the matter worse in this instance was, that it was Christmas Day that saw me go dinnerless.

The next day we returned to Tchelga, and prepared for our departure to Genda, which, being only at a distance of twenty miles, we reached the same evening. We were very hospitably received by Mr. Flad. Both he and Mrs. Flad speak very good English, and Mrs. Flad, having been a deaconess in the German establishment in Jerusalem, was consequently well acquainted with Arabic also. Her skilful management had succeeded in forming a very comfortable home, which was also enlivened by a pretty little girl, so that Abyssinia on the whole appeared to be rendered quite bearable. Alas! that after events should ever have marred the fair picture.

Genda is situated on a small elevation above the plain of Dembea, and the neighbourhood is the most fruitful part of any in the country. It is principally occupied by Falashas or native Jews, and the Scotch Jewish Mission had also a station a few miles off Genda, where I had the pleasure of finding Messrs. Steiger and Brandeis, two gentlemen whose acquaintance I had made in Alexandria. Mr. Flad had induced some thirty Jews to embrace Christianity; but the laws of the country will not permit him to form a church of his own, so he was obliged to unite them to the native one. This would be going from bad to worse, did he not by precept and example succeed in keeping up in them a higher tone of feeling than that around them.

Not the least part of Mr. Flad's kindness to me during my stay was his presenting me with a change of raiment, my Khartoum outfit being now in the last stages of decay. I was now transformed into an Abyssinian, my dress consisting of full trousers and shirt and the cotton cloth called the *shamaa*. This last has a broad red border, and is worn like the Roman toga or Scotch plaid. To prevent it from being blown about by the wind, it is not uncommon to have a leopard-skin, cut into a peculiar shape, fastened above it. It is the male dress in Abyssinia: the female consists of a long cotton gown reaching to the ankles, and fastened with a cord round the waist.

Permission having been granted us to proceed, on New Year's Day, 1863, we left Genda for Debra Tabor, the residence of King Theodore. We soon entered the vast plain of Dembea, which is under the richest cultivation, and towards evening reached the northern shores of Lake Tsana. The lake, a beautiful and welcome sight to us, is situated some 6000 feet above the sea, and is about seventy miles in length by forty in breadth.

It appears to have originally occupied an extent much beyond this, which is shown by the flat alluvial plains of Dembea, Foggera, and Gojam—the lowering of the waters of which has laid bare a fruitful land to cultivation. Several beautiful islands lie on its smooth surface, covered with rich tropical foliage; yet, notwithstanding all its attractions, the Abyssinians have never built a boat on it worthy of the name. In addition to the teff, doura, wheat, barley, and other cereals, its shores produce a little cotton, the grape-vine, and a few fruit trees, such as the peach. In the south-west the coffee-plant is said also to flourish. Indeed, this country is capable of producing anything, for there is every variety of climate between the high mountain-lands and the deep lowlands and valleys. The River Arno, and other small streams which have their source in the mountains round Gondar, disembogue into Lake Tsana on its northern side; while at its north-east corner a rocky ridge of hills, separating Dembea from the province of Foggera, abuts into the lake, and is continued in a chain of small islands to a few miles from the shore. Hence the road conducts, over a somewhat rough country, to the flourishing market-town of Ifak, where we arrived on the third day. On leaving Ifak we descended into the

plain of Foggera, and soon after crossed the River Reb
by a stone bridge, made by the Portuguese. The stream
was then rather low, but during the heavier rains the
bridge itself is overflowed. In the plain of Foggera we
found it excessively hot, the sun's rays being reflected
upon us by the surrounding mountains. A few hours
beyond the Reb we began to ascend the steep range of
mountains which culminate in Debra Tabor, leaving
on our right an isolated hill, called Eagle's Rock, from
the vast number of those birds which make their nests
in its higher clefts. Our ascent, though steep, was
easy, there being here some semblance of a road, the
work, I believe, of the Workmen's Mission. The views
from the higher parts of the mountain were exceedingly
fine, and I could not help once exclaiming to the consul,
in allusion to a previous occupation of my own, "This
is far superior to scribbling in a Bank." He laughed
heartily, and said, "Immeasurably." A few hours
more over an undulating country brought us to the
European colony of Gaffat, situated a little below the
high summit of Mount Tabor.

CHAPTER VI.

GAFFAT.

The Workmen's Mission—Bishop Gobat, Herr Spittler, and Dr. Krapf — Visit of inquiry — Maderakal — Satisfactory account— Departure of the Mission—Well received by the king—Road-making — Construction of mortars — Difficulties and failures— Final success and reward—Christian labours—Religion of Abyssinia—Abuna, or patriarch—Priests and monks—Churches and church decorations—Ludicrous paintings—Life, death, and judgment of a cannibal—Kissing the church—Feasts and fasts—Tecla Haimanot—The devil and the wonderful boa-constrictor—Estimate of Abyssinian character.

When, in 1838, Bishop Gobat felt necessitated to relinquish the English Church Mission in Abyssinia, his interest in that far-off country by no means ceased with his departure, but, on the contrary, his earnest desire was the projection of some scheme for its welfare and prosperity. His continued intercourse with Abyssinian pilgrims at Jerusalem no doubt also tended to keep alive this interest, and the result was the formation of a plan, in which he was materially assisted by Mr.

Spittler, the eminent Christian philanthropist at Basle, for sending to that country a number of artisans and tradesmen, whose object should be the gaining of an honest livelihood, at the same time that they were to do their utmost, by teaching and example, to raise the people to a higher degree of Christianity and civilisation. For this purpose, in the year 1854, six young men were chosen from among the pupils of St. Chrischona Institute at Basle, and sent to Jerusalem to receive some preliminary instruction in Amharic previous to their departure for Abyssinia.

It was about this time that Dr. Krapf, who had been on a visit to Europe for the benefit of his health, was about to return to his post at Rabbai Mpia, on the east coast of Africa; and as he also took a lively interest in the welfare of Abyssinia, having previously laboured some years in the country, he now proposed to revisit it on his way with one of the young men of the Workmen's Mission, the object being to investigate the political state of the country and calculate the feasibleness of a residence there. Mr. Flad, our friend of Genda, was the one appointed by Bishop Gobat for this object, and with the doctor left Jerusalem in December, 1854, for Cairo. Here they were joined by a young Abyssi-

nian named Maderakal, of whose history, as I shall
have occasion to mention him afterwards, I will give a
short account as told to me by himself.

When a mere lad he was engaged as a servant by
M. Lefèvre, a French traveller in Abyssinia, by whom,
with the consent of his parents, he was taken to France
to be educated. Here he was presented by M. Guizot
to King Louis Philippe, who showed him several
marks of favour, presenting him with a purse of money,
&c. He was placed at school in Paris, and while there
attracted the attention of the Jesuits, who thought that,
if properly instructed, he might form a useful propa-
gandist of their tenets in Abyssinia, a country which,
ever since the fifteenth century, had been the scene of
their oft-renewed but yet unsuccessful labours. These
religionists represented to the monarch the desirable-
ness of Maderakal's being made their pupil. Somewhat reluctantly, for he had perhaps destined him to
be a French political rather than religious agent, the
king finally relinquished him into their hands. He
was now removed to the Jesuit College, where they
began to initiate him into the rites of the sacred office
which he was destined to fulfil. But Maderakal would
not learn his genuflexions, and continued pressure being

brought to bear on him, the result was he ran away. He was now taken up by his old master Lefèvre, who carried him off to Egypt. While here Lefèvre wished him to sign a paper, the contents of which he would not allow him to see. Maderakal stoutly objected to do it, which occasioned a great want of accord between them. By obtaining ingress into M. Lefèvre's room while that person was absent, Maderakal examined the paper, and found that it was an agreement binding him to engage, on arrival at his own country, to find 500 Abyssinians to be sent to Bourbon. Terrified and enraged Maderakal complained to the French consul, who removed him from M. Lefèvre's charge. He now found an entrance into the school of Mr. Lieder, Church Missionary at Cairo, whence he was received into the Malta College, where he remained four years. He then went to England, and lived there two years; and it was on his return from this country that he came across Dr. Krapf and Mr. Flad at Cairo, and agreed to accompany them to his native land.

On the 20th of February they arrived safely at Massowa, whence they proceeded to Debra Tabor. Here they had an interview with Theodore, then newly constituted king, as well as with the Abuna or patriarch, both of whom expressed their willingness to receive the mission—Theodore on account of the benefit to be derived from European artisans, the Abuna from the respect which he affected towards the Protestant missionaries. Their object being thus gained, they returned to Europe to make the necessary arrangements, Dr. Krapf being unable to continue his journey to East Africa.

In the meanwhile Maderakal remained in his native Adowa, and there commenced holding a school, in which he instructed a dozen or two of boys out of the Amharic Bible. He was not allowed, however, to continue this work long, but was called for by the king to act as interpreter in European languages. The king also thought that he would have brought back a useful acquaintance with European arts and sciences after an eleven years' residence abroad; but in this he was disappointed, for Maderakal evinced but a very slight mechanical knowledge, which was rather the fault of his instructors than his own. He has since been retained in presence of the king, and his figure in recent events has not been unimportant.

In the beginning of 1855, Mr. Flad, now married, and accompanied by Messrs. Bender, Kiensle, Mayer,

and two German gunsmiths, again commenced the
journey, and after much hardship and sickness, to which
the two gunsmiths succumbed, finding untimely graves
at Wekhni, they arrived in the king's camp, who received them very kindly. They accompanied him in
his military campaigns, busying themselves for the most
part in road-making. For this purpose the king gave
them some hundreds of the natives, and the result is
seen in a decidedly improved condition of some of the
more frequented routes. It is said that this improvement commenced in a very simple manner. They were
riding one day with the king in the front of his army
when they came upon a route which was covered with
large stones and boulders, making it very difficult and
unpleasant for the mules. The Europeans were induced
to make a remark to the effect that in their country
such a state of things would not be allowed to exist.
Without more ado the king leaped from his mule, and
commenced picking up the shattered pieces of rock
and casting them to the side of the way. As the king
had dismounted, not a man in the army dared retain
his seat. Taking the hint given by their sovereign,
they commenced one and all to clear away the boulders
which lay thickly scattered over the path, so that in an

incredibly short space of time a road of some miles in extent was rendered for the future comparatively clear and easy. On another occasion Theodore did not even need a reminder from the Europeans. He chanced to come to a spot where the recent rains had cut away the soft soil and left a high embankment, that from its abruptness the horses and mules were unable to descend. He was on foot in a moment, and with his spear commenced digging away the earth in a manner that, with a little assistance, soon made the road passable.

In 1858 these Chrischona brethren were joined by Messrs. Waldmaier and Saalsmüller, also from that institution, and afterwards by M. Bourgaud, a French gunsmith, Herr Zander, a German, some time resident in Abyssinia, and Herr Moritz, a Polish soldier, who had deserted from the Russian army and come into Abyssinia as an adventurer. Mr. Flad afterwards put himself into communication with the London Society for the Promotion of Christianity amongst the Jews, and removed to Genda; the rest, in compliance with the wish of the king, settled in Gaffat, within a mile or two of Debra Tabor, where the king generally resides. Here each worked at his respective trade, for which they got well paid by the king, and things

went on smoothly for some time, until one day an
order came from his Majesty to the effect that he
wished them at once to commence the construction of
mortars and bombshells. The order came upon them
like the bursting of a bomb itself, for none of them
had ever had an idea that they would have been required to undertake work of that description. They of
course demurred, informing the king that, not having
learnt the founding of cannon, they were totally unpre-
pared to enter into an engagement of that description,
and that if he really desired to have these war implements in his country, manufacturers in either Germany,
England, or France would supply him with a much
better article than they could possibly produce. The
king was dissatisfied with their reply: he wished to
have these things made in his own country, and to be
quite independent of other nations. They still, nevertheless, objected, more on the ground of inability than
unwillingness; but their refusal only vexed the king
more, and he now seized all their servants and put
them in chains, there to remain until their masters gave
consent to carry out his will. In their perplexity they
could not do otherwise than promise to try. Only one of
them, Herr Moritz, could be said to have the slightest

acquaintance with the work at all, and his knowledge only extended to the formation of the mould; the clay to be used in the construction of fire-bricks, the formation of the furnace, the proportion of the metals, and the making of the fusee, being equally unknown to him as to the rest. However, by putting their heads together, and seeking information from books, they eventually managed to turn out something. What? A mass of vitreous matter formed by the melting of the fine sand of the bricks; the metal refused to flow. Their only resource was to try again; and away they went over the country to seek better fire-brick clay, and now another venture was made. The result was a flow of metal that came pouring out in a molten stream now, and all hearts are hopeful that at last their object is gained; but alas! the metal had stopped, and the mould was only half full. They tried again. To the inexpressible joy of these persevering men, and the intense delight of the king himself, their wishes are accomplished, and Debra Tabor for the first time saw the balls soaring up into the air and bursting with a loud crash, which made the hills resound with a hundred echoes.

This success was the cause of great favour being

conferred by the grateful king on his " children," as he called them. Shirts of honour, horses and mules with gold and silver trappings, and 1000 dollars apiece, were the reward of their persevering efforts. These gentlemen also maintain that by thus obeying the commands of the king they rescued their own mission, as well as that of the London and Scottish Jewish Societies, from the ruin which at that time seemed to threaten them. Be this as it may, they had afterwards full permission from his Majesty, who had taken a good deal of the spiritual as well as temporal rule into his own hands, to preach and teach to the natives, as well as to hold services in Amharic, the language of Abyssinia, at their own homes.

Abyssinia is said to have been converted to Christianity in the beginning of the fourth century by Frumentius, a native of Tyre, who was shipwrecked on its shores. Carried captive to the court of the then reigning queen, he used the opportunity given him for extending the new faith. He was afterwards appointed by Athanasius, patriarch of Alexandria, to be its first bishop or Abuna (our father). Since then the church of Abyssinia has maintained an uninterrupted connection with the Coptic church, receiving to this day its Abuna from

Egypt. The Abuna has the appointing of priests and other church officers. The ceremony is performed by laying on of hands. Priests that are already married have the privilege of entering the sacred office, but none must marry afterwards. Their duties consist in reading the prayers, chanting, administering the sacraments, and dancing, the latter being indulged in during religious processions, and consisting of a peculiar swaying to and fro of the body rather than a free use of the legs. Upon them also devolves the duty of instructing youth, but not exclusively, for there is another class called *debteras* or learned men, who are schoolmasters as well as scribes. Some monasteries are found in different parts, but nuns, I believe, are rare.

The churches are generally built on the summit of hills in the midst of cypress groves. They are round, with conical roofs, and divided after the Jewish model into three parts. The outer court is open, being the space between the wall and the posts supporting the roof, which extends about four yards beyond the main building. The second part, corresponding with the Holy Place, is the space between the outer wall and another which encloses the holiest of all; and here the people congregate for Divine worship. The holiest is

only entered by the priest, and contains what is called
the *tabot* or ark, in which the sacred vessels and books
are kept. The exterior of this enclosure is profusely
painted with sacred and historical subjects by native
artists, which, to an European, are subjects of great
amusement. Michael the Archangel and St. George
and the Dragon nearly always occupy the door. In
representations of the future world it is remarkable
that they always paint angels and good men white,
devils and bad men black, which on one occasion made
me ask a priest by way of a joke whether all Abyssinians, being black, went to the nether world. Anomalies
are common as in mediæval art. The Philistines appear
to have known the use of the blunderbuss, and the
Lord's Supper seems to have been conducted in the same
manner as an Abyssinian feast. One representation
amused me much. It represented the life, death, and
judgment of a man who had been a cannibal. Tableau
the first showed the monster in the act of demolishing
sundry human arms and legs. Tableau the second, the
same individual bestowing alms on the poor on Friday,
the fast day. Tableau the third, his death and coming
to judgment, in which Christ is represented with a pair
of scales, one of which is filled with the man's canni-

balism, the other with his fasting and almsgiving, the latter having a slight preponderance. Tableau the fourth represents the devil disputing with Mary the justice of the decision, and forcibly asserting his claim by seizing the individual in question by the leg, the Virgin maintaining her hold of the head. Tableau the fifth, triumph of Mary, and the quondam cannibal's admission to paradise.

Sometimes the tolling of a bell, but in most cases the beating of kettledrums, summons the faithful to prayers. The prayers are read in Ethiopic, a language which the people know nothing about, so that little profit can be derived from the service. Indeed, most persons content themselves with kissing the floor or walls of the edifice, and such is a criterion of a man's piety ; "he kisses the church," they say, and so esteem him a good Christian. Some will utter a prayer. The petition takes a form similar to the following, which an old woman was heard to offer up during my visit, though the last clause is probably in most cases omitted :

"Oh Lord, give me plenty to eat and drink, good raiment, and a comfortable home, or else kill me out-right !"

The sacrament is administered in both kinds, only

that raisins are steeped in water to form the wine. Wine is scarce in the country. Baptism is administered by immersion every year. The rite of circumcision universally prevails.

Christian liberty is entirely unknown, as the people are bound down to unmeaning forms and ceremonies, and the observance of fasts which extend over two-thirds of the year. Their calendar is crammed full of saints, and the days of the year by no means suffice for them all, so that they have morning celebrations and evening celebrations. One cannot wonder at this when their latitudinarianism leads them to commemorate Balaam and his Ass, Pontius Pilate and his Wife, and such like doubtful saints. In addition to the heroes of the Bible and Apocryphal books, they have many local saints, who have at various times astonished Abyssinia by their miracles and prodigies, particularly one called Tecla·Haimanot, who usurps an importance in the Abyssinian mind often before Mary or even Jesus. He is said to have converted the devil, and induced him to become monk for forty days, though what became of him afterwards we are at a loss to know. I suppose that fasting and celibacy did not agree with him for longer than that term of trial, and therefore he became a "backslider." The same holy man, wishing to ascend a steep mountain with perpendicular sides, similar to the Guimb I have described, was accommodated in answer to prayer with a boaconstrictor, which took him up on its back.

Such is the bushel of error and fable beneath which the light of Christian truth is hid. Apart from such traditional excrescences, the Abyssinians are orthodox in their belief, the grand truths of our religion being received alike by them as by us; but being void of that charity which edifieth, their knowledge has only tended to puff them up, and the intolerance with which they look upon their Mohammedan and Jewish neighbours is even greater than that of those people themselves towards Christians; indeed, they often include in their contempt every form of Christianity even which does not conform to their own. The blue-neck thread, which is the distinguishing badge between them and Mohammedans and Jews, is their great glory, while they have forgotten the cultivation of those virtues which should be the distinctive characteristics of a Christian. What renders their pride the more offensive is that the Mohammedans and Jews are in every way their superiors, possessing with an equal amount of intelligence far greater mechanical genius and superior habits of industry. All the manufacturers of cotton cloths are Moslems; all the builders and artisans are Jews. But pride is not their only fault: they are deceitful, lying, insincere; their breasts are seldom stirred by generosity towards others, or in gratitude for benefits received; and, added to all, they are inhospitable, which in the estimation of even Mohammedans, whose ideas of morality and virtue are not as ours, is a great offence. Hospitality will redeem the character of an Arab, but an Abyssinian cannot even boast of this.

It will be seen from the above remarks that I find it difficult to lay my finger on any good quality in the Abyssinian; but, lest I should be uncharitable, I may say that in my experience of Orientals, as a general rule, I have found that a deeper knowledge of them is attended with a due moderation of the harsh judgment one is too apt to form of their character on a merely slight acquaintance. Having only had six months' intercourse with them, I feel bound to leave the *Credit side* open for those travellers who have had longer experience of them to fill up—if so be they are able.

CHAPTER VII.

DEBRA TABOR.

German colony of Gaffat—Our kind welcome—Arrival of the king
—My reception at Court—Description of his Majesty—Expert
equestrian — Warlike preparations — Consuls in Abyssinia — A
slight incident—Trial of mortars—Strange contrasts in King
Theodore's character—Good qualities—Fondness for children—
The King's Own—His reception of French consul—Indifference to
presents—What the king thought of box-organs—Kind treatment
of the author.

ON our arrival at Gaffat we went immediately to the
house of Mr. Waldmaier, as we had been recommended
to do by Mr. Flad. Mr. Waldmaier received us with
the most Christian hospitality, and afterwards introduced us to the other members of the community.
These gentlemen have adopted the Abyssinian mode of
living and dress, and some of them have married native
ladies. Others have been more fortunate in securing
for wives the half-caste daughters of Europeans, Mr.
Waldmaier, our host, among the number, he being

united to Miss Bell, the daughter of the well-known Englishman who was general in the king's army. Their dwelling-places are the conical huts of the country, which are all situated in a clump on the summit of a gentle hill. It is the invariable custom in these regions to build towns and villages on heights, probably to secure an advantageous position, as affording some slight defence against the attack of an enemy, and also for sanitary reasons. Inasmuch as all the architects of Abyssinia are Jews, and indeed the nation itself partly of Jewish extraction, it may also be that this is a relic of the custom of "setting a city on a hill" which prevailed amongst the ancient Israelites. A church, moreover, is never erected but in these prominent positions. We may suppose it to be in traditional remembrance of the "mountain of the Lord's House." This Jewish origin or admixture of blood in the Abyssinians is also shown by a fondness for naming places from parts of the Holy Land : Debra Tabor (Mount Tabor), Debra Libanos (Mount Lebanon), Antiokia (Antioch), are examples.

Our little company was afterwards joined by Mr. Hausmann, on a visit from Matammah for the benefit of his impaired health, and also by a French military surgeon whom M. Lejean had left at Khartoum sick. We now formed a company of a dozen, and in such society the time passed away very agreeably.

The king was absent when we arrived. He was then in the camp, some three days' journey to the south. A week, however, had scarcely elapsed before his return to Debra Tabor was announced, and then, as is customary, all the Europeans turned out to greet him. I being a commoner, it was not thought necessary to arrange any formalities for my presentation to his Majesty; indeed, had it been left to myself, I should willingly have avoided an immediate interview with Theodore; but I was told that it was impossible to hold back, the king insisting upon seeing all Europeans newly arrived in the country. Pending the construction of his new palace, he at that time occupied a large conical hut, which only differed from the generality of its kind in its ample dimensions and its possession of a large chandelier suspended from the centre of the roof. It was thought desirable that I should remain outside till the rest had entered, and paid their respects to his Majesty on his safe return; Mr. Waldmaier, who acted as my *balderabba* or introducer, then informing him that a young Englishman awaited the honour of an intro-

duction. The king instantly gave command for me
to be admitted, which was communicated to me by a
native; so doffing my hat and shoes, leaving the latter
on the threshold, I made a bold advance into the
interior of the hut; but great was my surprise when,
instead of finding anywhere the outward paraphernalia
of Oriental royalty, I beheld the famous Theodore, the
renowned warrior and absolute lord of a great dominion,
dressed in plain cotton shirt and trousers, and these not
over-clean, seated, not on a throne, but on a low divan
raised about a foot from the ground. Thinking at first
that it could not be the king himself who was seated
before me, the profound bow with which I entered was
rather uncertainly directed. His request by indication
that I would be seated reassured me, and, doubling my
legs up in the Oriental manner, I squatted down among
the rest. We were now well supplied with arracky and
tedge (honey-wine) in the drinking line, as well as with
a plain breakfast of teff bread and stewed meat to
satisfy the more solid demands of hunger. In the
meanwhile the king, who was sipping arracky all the
time,* chatted away very pleasantly in Amharic with

---

* I here take occasion to remark that, though Theodore consumes
a vast quantity of arracky, he is no drunkard; that is, I have never

the missionaries, plying them with questions in theology, or discussing their recent successes in mortar-making.

His appearance was that of a man of about forty-five, of middling stature, and possessed of a well-knit but not over-powerful frame, conveying more the idea of being tough and wiry than of strong physical development. His complexion is dark, approaching to black,

---

heard of him being overcome with drink. He always stops at a certain point. His usual drink is the arracky of the Soudan, made from dates, honey, &c. The idea which has got about of this being the sole distillation of the artisans of Gaffat is simply preposterous, and Dr. Beke ought to have been the last person to have hinted at such a thing, for, having studied Bruce, he might have known that not only "excellent red wine," "honey-wine, or hydromel," "a species of beer, called bouza," but also "*strong, good, new brandy*," was a common drink of Abyssinia, even in his time. I have said before, that Balambaras Guelmo had abundance of arracky, as indeed have all those who can afford it. The Europeans found it in the country; and surely they were at liberty to make their own, especially when they found they could make it better than the natives. It is just possible that the king, on tasting theirs, found it better than his own, and so got them to make some for him; but if so, this would not be confined to the Chrischona brethren. Mr. Moritz, the Polish soldier, and Mr. Zander, an old resident, had the best that I tasted. Mr. Flad's also was excellent. So much for Mr. Layard's "brandy merchants" and Dr. Beke's "Book of Quinte Essence."

H

but he has nothing of the negro about him. His features
are altogether those of an European. His head is well
formed, and his hair is arranged in large plaits extending back from the forehead. The forehead is high, and
tends to be prominent. His eye is black, full of fire,
quick and piercing. His nose has a little of the Roman
about it, being slightly arched and pointed. His mouth
is perfect, and the smile, which during the conversation
continually played upon it, was exceedingly agreeable,
I may say fascinating. He has very little moustache
or beard. His manner was peculiarly pleasant, gracious,
and even polite, and his general expression, even when
his features were at rest, was one of intelligence and
benevolence. On the whole, the physiognomist would
find no trace of fierce passion save in the lightning
glance of his eyes. I watched for the keen shot of
light coming from them at times, and reflected upon
what he could be capable of, but they did not strike me
as treacherous eyes. I felt that he could act savagely
under irritation.

Our repast concluded, the king signified his intention
of visiting the foundry where his European workmen
had made the last mortar. He descended the hill bare-
footed and bareheaded, though the nature of the ground

was excessively rough, and covered with thorny bushes, and as it was noon the sun also was very hot; but shoes or hats are considered superfluities in Abyssinia. He requested us to mount our mules; of course, like thorough-bred courtiers, we refused to do this so long as he walked himself. My right shoe having a large hole in it that exposed two or three toes of my unstockinged foot, I cut myself so severely against a sharp stone that the blood began to flow pretty freely. Some dirt got into the wound, and inflammation ensued, occasioning me a painful sore, which it took a couple of months to heal.

Maderakal, of whom I have previously given an account, turned to good use the lessons in genuflexions he had received of the Jesuit priests in France, by running before the king, and at every few strides prostrating himself, as he demanded permission to go and see his relations at Adowa, whom he had not now beheld for some years. The king so far granted his request as to promise that when he had subjugated the rebel Tadla Gualoo in Gojam, and had no more need of his Tigrean soldiers, he would send him back with them to his native place. His assent to the petition was signified placably and kindly.

When we had reached the plain at the foot of Mount Tabor, Theodore mounted his horse. Agile and supple, he sprang off the ground into the saddle without touching the stirrup. He is so expert in this feat of horsemanship that he is said to be able to vault into his seat even while the horse is in motion, like the trained Arab. Evidently his pride animated him highly on horseback. We having also mounted, he then amused himself by chasing Maderakal with spear in hand over the plain. Off they flew. Maderakal was only riding a mule, but he skimmed along on it so swiftly and well that the king was highly gratified with him, and bought the mule of him there and then, giving of course a kingly price for it.

We now arrived at Gaffat, and here we were met by M. Lejean, who, hearing of the king's approach, had only time to assume his uniform before Theodore arrived. M. Lejean had wished to hoist the tricolour on the top of his tent, but he was dissuaded from it, as he was told that the king would be greatly displeased at such a course, as representing an encroachment on his prerogative. This objection is part and parcel of that which he entertains against the establishment of consulates in his dominions. The king's idea is

that the existence of no other power should be recognised in the country besides his own, and that all
persons residing in his territories, natives or foreigners,
must obey the laws of the land, and be subject to him
entirely. It is an instance of his singularly jealous
character, and of his view of despotism. If, therefore,
a consul ventures into the country, he must not do so
with the idea that his person will be considered sacred,
or that the power represented by him will impose awe ;
but he must be prepared to stand on the same footing
as a native of the country. Hence the subsequent
imprisonment of the French and English consuls, in
whatever light we may choose to regard it, was not
looked upon by Theodore as an infringement of the
rights of nations; for rights of this nature he had
never recognised. I believe, however, with regard to
ambassadors the case is different, and that the custom
of ancient nations in respect to them holds good in
Abyssinia; at all events, the persons of messengers
passing between two contending armies are held sacred.

The consul seemed at first as uncertain to whom to
make obeisance as I had been myself, for several of his
Majesty's nobles being dressed in gay-coloured tunics,
the king appeared the last person of all to be the one

who claimed regal honours. M. Lejean's hesitation,
however, was but momentary, for a word from one of
the Europeans soon enabled him with a profound bow
to tender homage where homage was due. The king
merely responded with a few words of welcome, and
then asked the consul when he would wish to be
received officially. M. Lejean of course made answer
that it would be when it should please his Majesty.
The king accordingly appointed the day following. His
manner was familiar, not imperious in any degree.

He now passed on to the enclosure where the last
mortar had been turned out, and proceeded at once to
inspect the furnace, while the various processes were
explained to him by his " children."

During this ceremony a slight incident happened to
myself which might have brought me into trouble. The
enclosure which contained the furnace was surrounded
by a light framework of bamboos. It happened that I
was following some few yards behind the king; my foot
slipped, and I fell against the framework in such a
manner that the end of a long bamboo flying back
struck his Majesty on the back of the head. Nobody
appeared to have noticed the affair but the king. He
faced about quietly, and gave me a mild glance. I

suspect that he must have guessed at once how I had blundered. It was a very peculiar, benevolent, transitory look. I translated it as implying forgiveness readily. What grieved me most was, that the great crush of people prevented me from getting sufficiently near to ask his pardon. He seemed to have forgotten the circumstance immediately after.

The king now expressed a wish to see a few bombs fired from the recent issue of his foundry, and we all accordingly adjourned to the courtyard of Mr. Saalsmüller's house, which offered the best advantages for the object in view. A carpet was brought out and spread upon the ground, on which his Majesty seated himself, and he also bade M. Lejean be seated on the same. The remainder of us squatted down where we could find room, Europeans occupying the inner circle. The mortar was brought out and placed, though not fastened, in its carriage; when it was duly loaded and primed Mr. Bender was deputed to fire it. The trial on the whole was very successful, though, as the mortar had not been fastened, it kicked to such an extent as to fly a few feet out of its carriage, to the imminent danger of Mr. Bender. While these bombs were being fired the king seemed buried in deep thought; his head was bent, he spoke to no one about him ; I did not see that he opened his lips at all. I had begun to watch him curiously, and I was much struck by this profoundly meditative expression that had come on him. The fit lasted until the experiments had ceased ; he then looked round, and fixing his eyes sharply on one who sat near him, fell into animated conversation on the subject of artillery. All the Europeans joined in this conversation. The king said that he desired to have still larger bombs made, for which purpose he would build them extensive workshops, and supply, to any amount they wished, the metal required in their manufacture.

All the time that Theodore was speaking of these warlike preparations, he was playing with a little child of M. Bourgaud's, which he had seated alongside of him on the carpet, between himself and M. Lejean ; and, certainly, a stranger who saw him then for the first time, and who knew nothing of his antecedents, would have found it difficult to believe that he was the cruel monster which recent accounts unite in describing him. But there is a strange contradiction, a curious two-sidedness about King Theodore, which has sorely perplexed all who have endeavoured to form an estimate of his character. There are those who think they have described the man when they have stigmatised him as an inhuman despot, a bloodthirsty tyrant, a Nero, a worse than King of Dahomey. Considering the sufferings which some who thus characterise him have endured at his hands, we scarcely like to dispute the judgment; but experience is not to be trusted implicitly as a guide to character. After all, they may only be looking at one side of him—the side which he presents for the moment to them. Others, like myself, have been well treated by him; and, considering that he could have had no motive for thus treating us but pure kindness, we are bound to testify so far in his favour. Our testimony may not go a long way, but such as it is let it stand. He seems just now to have great need of it.

No, Theodore is not all devil! else how comes it that those who have known him best and longest have given the most favourable account of him? Take Bell, for instance, who was his bosom companion, and Plowden, his friend, who both lost their lives in his service. It would be a poor tribute to their memory to say that they gave a life's devotion to one who was no better than a King of Dahomey. They must have seen, or fancied they saw, something good in him—something of a white, as well as a black, side to his character. And perhaps, in pity for human nature, it would be as well if we also could see a little of this light side, after we have got sickened (as we all have) with the dark.

When I beheld the arm of this warrior-king—this man who had slain his thousands and tens of thousands —thrown, in a fond caress, round the little child of the white man, I felt that Theodore must have tenderness lying in him somewhere. His passion for children was confirmed to me by several testimonies. I was told that he has always adopted, as a kind of King's Own, all children born during a campaign, and has charged himself with their education and bringing up. Shakespeare tells us we should distrust the man who is never stirred by the harmony of sweet sounds—and, he might have added by the sight of childhood's innocence; and if the converse of the latter holds good, he who is interested in a little child, because it is a child, is, to say the least, human.

On the following day his Majesty gave a formal reception to the French consul. He received him with the discharge of cannon, and seated in state. This latter ceremonious position consisted in his being perched up on the top of a high wall, hung with gay carpets and coloured cloths, the whole surface of the ground round about being also spread with the same. He expressed his approbation of Napoleon's letter, proposing friendship, which M. Lejean had brought, and signified his earnest desire to be on friendly relationship with France, just the same as he was with England; and said he had already sent a letter to the Emperor of France as well as to the Queen of England, expressing his desire to send ambassadors to both countries, and inquiring whether they could ensure the safe passage of these through the Turkish dominions, with the Sultan of which he was then not on good terms. The consul assured him, on the part of his government, that there would be no difficulty on the score of the Turks, and that either European power was sufficiently strong to ensure the safe conveyance of his ambassadors through Egypt. The consul now ordered his servants to bring forward the presents, consisting of revolvers, pistols, &c., richly mounted, and several boxes containing rich silks, muslins, &c., specimens of Lyons manufacture. Unlike most African potentates, and as if to prove how mistaken general conceptions of him are, he did not display the least anxiety to behold these

gifts of Napoleon. He did not look at them disdain-
fully, but without interest in them, remarking, in an
unconcerned way, after a short inspection, that friendship was far better than presents. Catching sight of
the revolvers, at a second glance, he took them in his
hands and examined them with the eye of one accustomed to their use; but he uttered no comment or
exclamation, and quickly returned them to the hands of
his attendants. As regards the silks, he did not even
wait to see the bottom of the boxes which contained
them, before he bundled them off to the apartments of
the queen. Such things could only be meant for women!
Some coloured pictures, however, on the lids of the
boxes for a moment seemed to interest and amuse him,
especially one containing a representation of an indig-
nant farmer receiving with a pitchfork a suspicious
character who was making his exit from the window of
his wife's bedroom. Captain Cameron, our own consul,
had not been much more fortunate than M. Lejean in
the choice of some of his presents; for on presenting,
amongst other things, a box organ, the king said,
" What's the good of you Europeans bringing me these
nonsensical things ?" and consigned it at once to obli-
vion in the house of Mr. Waldmaier.

These mistakes need never have been made, for Mr. Plowden had long before expressly stated, that Theodore "regarded nothing with pleasure or desire but munitions of war for his soldiers." One or two small field-pieces, some stands of arms, a few barrels of gunpowder, or a quantity of percussion-caps, would have been sure to have pleased him. The French were excusable in making the mistake, but we were not. Theodore imagined that we trifled with him.

At the conclusion of M. Lejean's interview, the king asked him whether he wished immediately to depart for his post at Massowah, or would prefer staying in his country a short time? M. Lejean said he would prefer to stay; and the arrangements for the exercise of the king's hospitality were made.

Mr. Waldmaier then told the king my object in coming into this part of Africa, namely, with the hope of reaching the Galla countries to the south. At this the king smiled and shook his head, and then said:

"I am afraid the present unsettled state of the country will not possibly allow of your travelling therein, but when I have conquered the countries to the south, which originally belonged to my ancestors, then those parts will be open and safe to European travellers."

Traveller.—I must inform your Majesty that I my-self have been compelled to relinquish the idea for the present; for having been robbed in the country of the Arabs, I am now under the necessity of putting myself in communication with my own countrymen, either in India or England.*

King.—If you absolutely wish to go, I will supply you with a guide to Massowah; but if you are inclined to remain in my country, I will furnish you with every-thing you require.

Traveller (with a profound bow).—Your Majesty overwhelms me with kindness. If I thought I could in any way be of service to your Majesty, I would will-ingly remain.

King.—Do you understand the manufacture of gun-powder and percussion-caps?

Traveller.—No, I am sorry to say, I do not; in my own country I was brought up to the duties of a clerk.

King.—Well, I have often thought I would like to have an English secretary, if you are willing to become such.

---

* This remark was also necessary in order to explain why I had brought no presents, according to the general custom of travellers.

This was the English rendering Mr. Waldmaier gave to the word, but what was exactly meant by it I do not know. At this stage the conversation was interrupted; but whatever may have been the king's idea, I heard no more about the matter during my stay, and, perhaps, it was fortunate I did not.

During the course of the interview Mr. Waldmaier had gratuitously informed the king that I had walked a good part of the road; on hearing which he said he would present me with a mule. In the course of an hour or two a stout mule arrived at the door of my hut for me, ready equipped with the saddle and trappings of a native chief, so that my respectability was made at once.

CHAPTER VIII.

Theodore's history—Birth and parentage—Claims royal lineage—
Claim disputed — Real name Kassa — The coming Theodore —
Ambitious projects—A true patriot—A Crusader—Has his fortune
told—Mother sells kosso—He enters a convent—Escapes mas-
sacre—Enters the army—Attacks the Turks—Incites the jealousy
of Waisero Menin—Defeats her army—Is defeated by the Turks
—Fresh quarrel with the Waisero—Takes her prisoner—Becomes
Dejage of Dembea—Defeated by Birru Goshu—Seeks safety in
flight—Renews the attack—Kills Birru Goshu—Excites the fears
of Ras Ali—Victory of Aichal—Conquers Gojam—Defeats Oubie
—Is crowned king—Conquers the Wollo Gallas—Annexes Shoa—
His leniency to the conquered.

THE Emperor Theodore, "King of the Kings of Ethiopia"
(his title engraved on the royal seal), was born about the
year 1820 at Sherlia, a large village of Kuara, the most
western province of Abyssinia. His father, Aylo Walda
Georgis, younger brother to Dejage Comfou, chief of the
province, was of an illustrious family; and his mother,
by name Aitetegeb, could even boast a royal lineage,
tracing her descent, according to the king's own account,

from Menilek, son of Solomon, by Makada, Queen of Sheba, and founder of the Abyssinian dynasty. This claim, put forward by Theodore, has been much called in question by his enemies even amongst his own people; and a Mohammedan Abyssinian, who was "Army Tailor" to Agow Negusie, and whose acquaintance I made in Cairo, told me that, so far from Aitetegeb being of royal lineage, or even lawful wife to Walda Georgis, she was in reality nothing more than a camp follower, and that the only intimacy the chief ever had with her was when, in her capacity of scavenger, she would enter his tent to remove rubbish; the result being the present occupier of the Abyssinian throne. This story has so much of malicious slander on the face of it that it almost refutes itself.

Another report says that when, as a simple warrior chief, he had conquered all his enemies, he requested the priests to crown him king; and that they, having demurred on the ground of his not being of the royal family, he exclaimed, angrily, "Search the books!" which doing, behold! they found his kingly genealogy. Now, without attempting to cast a doubt on the truth of the sacerdotal order in Abyssinia, though we have had some very naughty jests amongst ourselves, it seems rather strange that these learned and wise men had not discovered this before he came to power, for some wicked people might say that fear had lent them clearer eyes than they generally possessed.

I mentioned to Mr. Waldmaier my having heard the report, but he said there was no reason to doubt the lawfulness of Theodore's claims; and Mertcha, who was some time Abyssinian dragoman at the British Consulate, solemnly assured me of the king's right, saying, that the genealogy could easily be traced to King Joas, who reigned in the time of Bruce, and so to Menilek. It may also be observed, that in a country whose population does not extend to four millions, and where the kings have been allowed a plurality of wives from time immemorial, it would be difficult to say who is not connected laterally, if not directly, with a dynasty which dates back some three thousand years. More numerous than the green-turbaned descendants of the Moslem prophet, the race of such a wholesale multiplier as Solomon may probably be found without as well as within the boundaries of Habesh.

The real name of the king is Kassa, he having assumed that of Theodoros, or Theodore, in reference to an Abyssinian prophecy, that an individual bearing this name is to arise in the latter days, and after restoring the ancient glory of the Ethiopian empire, pursue a course of conquest, having for his object the destruction of Mecca, and the rescuing of Jerusalem from the hands of the infidel. None other than this was the ambitious programme Theodore made out for himself.

The precise time at which he took up with these ideas perhaps he only is able to say, but Mr. Plowden informs us that " from his earliest youth he regarded his present elevation as assuredly destined." The probability is, therefore, that having once found out the fact of his royal descent, with that ambitious vanity which is the peculiarity of the Abyssinian, and the natural inheritance of a chieftain's son, he immediately sought to work his aspirations into a well-digested plan. Having early the advantage of a good education, his studies must have shown him that, while Abyssinian history pointed back to David, king of Israel, as the perfection of kings in the past, Abyssinian prophecy pointed forward to the coming Theodore as the perfect king of the future. Hence, while seeking to accomplish (however illogically) in his own person the prophecies regarding the latter, he took for a standard—a model to which he should conform himself—his illustrious progenitor, King David. With this idea he made the Israelitish king his study, always carrying on his person the Book of Psalms, and he not only found a parallel in his own history and that of David, but in similar circumstances used the very language of the latter, and this both to God and man. There was no blasphemy in this proceeding, nor hypocrisy; he was perfectly sincere. His desire was father to his belief. Seeing his country in ruins, he desired to save it, and so believed he was destined to be its saviour. His father's and uncle's contests with the advancing power of Egypt on the western frontiers, in which he himself was also engaged, had shown him the source of his country's crippled state and that which threatened its utter destruction. What was this?—Mohammedanism. Therefore Mohammedanism must disappear from his country; and not only so, he would wipe it off the face of the earth. A wild thought, no doubt; but, after all, not to be condemned as worse than patriotism run mad. His reveries in the presence of experimental guns were doubtless full of this vision. Theodore is the first and only patriot Abyssinia ever saw, and, assuredly, will be the last. This virtue, as Plowden has before observed, is entirely unknown to his countrymen; hence Theodore was never understood by them, and to this may be attributed his fall.

But Theodore's hatred to El-Islam was not only inspired by patriotism; it was fed and increased by the deep religiousness of his character. In him the spirit of the old Crusaders was strong. It is related of him that when a missionary once showed him a stereoscopic view of Jerusalem, the king asked, "What is this large building with dome and spire?"

"The Mohammedan mosque of Omar," replied the missionary.

The king leaned his head on his hand and began to weep. Then lifting his face he asked, angrily:

· "How is it that the powerful nations of England and France have suffered for so long the infidels to possess the Holy Land?"

He could never understand our Eastern policy in keeping the sick man "on his legs," and in the Crimean war his sympathies were rather with Russia. He even wrote to the Czar proposing a joint invasion of Syria for the extirpation of the Mohammedans; and having got snubbed in that quarter, as he had been everywhere else, he determined to undertake the task alone. In this purpose he was strengthened by the consideration that, as a lineal descendant of King David, in the line of Menilek, son of Solomon, he was justly entitled to occupy the throne of his ancestors. Through the Queen of Sheba he laid claim to all the territory originally included in Cush or Ethiopia, consisting of Abyssinia with its boundaries extended to Egypt on the north, and Zanzibar on the south, and Arabia, including the holy cities of Mecca and Medina; and through Solomon he claimed the whole of the Holy Land from the Euphrates to the Mediterranean. He thought he had a divine right to all these countries, and that the God of David, his father, would support him in it.

Having once got an inkling as to the scheme of a brilliant imperial destiny, he had recourse to "prophets and fortune-tellers" to have it confirmed. The result was no doubt favourable to his views. M. Lejean, in his "Théodore II. et le Nouvel Empire d'Abyssinie," gives an instance in which he thus had recourse to the supernatural. But seeing that M. Lejean obtained his information from those who were inimical to Theodore, the case has received a certain colouring from the narrators, which, while it destroys its credibility, has added not a little to its interest. I give it here in the words of M. Lejean:

"Towards the close of the year 1854 an officer, named Kassa, encamped with a body of cavalry in a plain on the borders of Lake Tsana. Followed by a page and two horsemen, he approached the lake; and, having arrived within thirty paces of its margin, made sign to his men to withdraw; then pursuing his way alone, he stopped on the shore of the lake and pronounced a few words of magic import. Immediately a thick cloud rose up from the liquid surface of the lake and revealed, on dissipating into the surrounding atmosphere, a troop of Shangalla (negroes) in the act of erecting a throne. This done, another Shangalla of formidable aspect, and having a crown upon his head, rose up from the lake and seated himself upon the throne; then fixing his gaze upon the officer, who all this time had not moved, he said, 'Thou hast called me forth from the abyss, dost thou know who I am?'

"'Yes,' replied the officer, 'I know thou art the Prince of Evil Spirits, but that is not the object of my summoning thee. Shall I be king?'

"'Thou wilt have a troubled and chequered life,' said the genii.

"'I do not ask thee that;—shall I be king?'

"'*Thou wilt*,' replied the demon, and immediately

disappeared with his throne and his slaves in a thick
cloud.

"Kassa, buried in deep thought, returned to his men
who had thus been made witnesses of this strange
scene."

I will now proceed with an account of the main
incidents in the king's life.

On the death of his father, Kassa was removed by
his mother to Gondar, where he received the rudiments
of his education. Here, however, the poor lady was so
reduced in circumstances as to be compelled to resort
to the sale of *kosso* in the market-place as a means of
subsistence. This barely sufficing for her own wants,
her youthful son found an entrance into a convent at
Tchangar, a village to the north-west of Lake Tsana,
and here he received that knowledge of religious questions and that insight into monastic life which he
turned to such good account afterwards. How long he
would have remained here it is difficult to say, had not
an event taken place which turned his energies into a
course of life in which he was destined to attain such
eminence. This was no less than the sack of the
convent by Dejage Maro, a chief who laid claim to the
province of Dembea, in which it was situated, and who

cruelly put to the sword its inmates, regardless of their tender age ; the young Kassa only escaping by flight.

He now sought refuge with his uncle, Dejage Comfou, to whom, on arriving at the age of manhood, he offered his services as common soldier during that powerful chief's engagements with the advancing power of Egypt on the Blue River, and is said to have so gained the admiration of his uncle by his daring and valour as to have induced him to speak in highly honourable terms of his gallant youthful nephew to Ras Ali, the governor of Western Abyssinia.

The death of Comfou, and the consequent dissensions of his three sons over the inheritance, occasioned a state of anarchy in Kuara, which rendered it an easy prey to the Egyptians on the west, and to the ambitious designs of Birru Goshu, chief of Damot and Gojam, on the south, and while the former encroached more and more on the ill-defined boundary of Western Abyssinia, the latter invaded the country with a numerous army, and soon succeeded in subduing the greater part of the unhappy province to his sway. Kassa, who had taken the part of Garad, Comfou's eldest son, had in this campaign another of those narrow escapes which have so marked his eventful life, he having only evaded capture and probable death by seeking refuge with a peasant of Sarago, where, though surrounded by enemies, he held good his retreat for more than a month. At the end of that time he succeeded in making his escape to the western borders of his native province, where he gathered a few trusty followers around him, and made raids on the provinces of his Egyptian neighbours, finding subsistence for himself and friends in the booty thus obtained. He gradually extended these razzias to the more northern districts, and would occasionally make a sudden descent upon the Tokruri Mohammedans, until his name became a terror to all along the frontier.

The success which attended Kassa on these expeditions soon brought to his camp great numbers of brave soldiers, whom the love of adventure, or hatred to El-Islam, impelled to make common cause with the renowned warrior, until his increasing power excited the fear and enmity of the Waisero Menin, the mother of Ras Ali, who began to think that Kassa's formidable array threatened the independence of her own province of Dembea. She accordingly collected an army, with the object of crushing the power of the young upstart, before his increasing popularity should render that task difficult, if not impossible. She was, however, too late.

The fame of Kassa was already sufficiently great to unnerve the arm and strike terror to the heart of the army she sent against him, and the result was that the forces of Menin, almost without a blow being struck, turned in ignominious retreat. Menin was now obliged to cede the province of Dembea—the richest in Abyssinia—to the conqueror, and concluded a peace by bestowing on him the hand of Tsoobedje, daughter of Ras Ali.

In the meantime the Arabs of the north seized the opportunity afforded them by their redoubtable foe's absence. They began to make inroads into Abyssinian territory, with the double object of plunder and revenge. No sooner, however, had affairs been satisfactorily settled in Dembea, than Kassa again appeared on the scene. He effected a sudden descent on the market-place of Matammah, regaining the mountains with the booty thus easily won. A second expedition, however, ended rather disastrously to himself. On this occasion he penetrated as far as the river Rahhad, where he came in contact with two regiments of Egyptian troops, well-armed with muskets and possessing two field-pieces. These advantages on the side of his enemies did not, however, prevent Kassa from engaging, though his wild soldiers were for the most part armed but with sword and lance, the latter only being of any service, as the Egyptians were entrenched behind a thick hedge of thorny trees, thus preventing the Abyssinians from coming to close quarters. The result might have been foreseen. The spears and few guns in the hands of bad marksmen of Kassa's party were a poor match against the trained soldiers and cannon of the Turks; and Kassa, seeing the disadvantage, soon commanded a retreat, which he conducted with his usual skill. The enemy did not venture to follow in pursuit: they knew that to quit their ranks, and the protection of their cannon and thorny fence, was to ensure destruction at the hand of their more courageous foes.

Kassa himself was wounded in this engagement, and on his return had to put himself under the surgical skill of a native doctor at Tchangar. This individual claimed an ox as his fee, and the wounded chief sent to the neighbouring town of Gondar, to the Waisero Menin, for a supply. It was a modest demand; yet the Waisero, who, it appears, still retained her animosity to her former enemy, refused to comply. She sent him, on the contrary, an insulting message, and the *quarter* of an ox. Kassa was enraged. As soon as he had recovered from his wound sufficiently to take the saddle, he gathered round him his recently dismissed soldiers, their numbers increased by gathering throngs from his native Kuara, and gave the Waisero battle near the capital; the fortunes of the day showing in favour of the injured chieftain. The victory was succeeded by the capture of the Waisero herself, who now became the prisoner of the chief whose anger she had so justly incurred.

Ras Ali, son to Menin, and prince of the whole of Western Abyssinia, bethought him, and not prematurely, that affairs had assumed a serious aspect that required his own interference; but being then engaged in war with Oubie, prince of Tigre, the eastern portion of the country, he was necessitated to confine his course of action to negotiation only, the result of which was that Kassa agreed to liberate the royal mother on condition of his being allowed to retain the title of Dejage, or Governor, of Dembea, with Gondar for his seat of government. These terms Ras Ali was obliged to accept for the time being, but as soon as the cessation of hostilities allowed, he annulled the treaty, and proclaimed Kassa a rebel, calling upon Birru Goshu, governor of Gojam, to expel him, and offering the chieftainship of Dembea as a reward in case of success. Goshu proceeded to collect a large army, and gave battle to the forces of Kassa in the plains of Dembea; vastly inferior in numbers, Kassa lost the day, and became again a fugitive to his own native province of Kuara. This was in 1850. Here he is said to have remained in his retreat for more than a twelvemonth, unknown even to his friends, and eking out a miserable subsistence from the products of the chase and the wild fruits the country afforded. In 1851, however, he again emerged from exile; and, gathering around him large numbers of his faithful Kuaranyas, resolved to contest again his right to the governorship of Dembea.

He now made a sudden descent on the army of Birru Goshu, encamped on the borders of Lake Tsana, between Genda and Tchangar. Again the superior forces of the enemy would have snatched the victory from him, had not an event occurred which was the turning-point of his fortunes. Kassa's own small force had already been routed by the enemy, and he himself, with a handful of his followers, had sought the protection afforded by a field of the lofty doura, or maize, when a horseman rushed by, clothed in the shirt of honour which marks the dignity of chief. Kassa, perceiving from his hiding-place that his foe was in his hands, drew a pistol from his girdle and fired; the ball entering his enemy's brain. Then rushing forward, he tore from the dead man his embroidered shirt, covered with blood, and carrying it aloft on his spear, collected the remnant of his army and charged afresh his terror-stricken foes, who, their leader slain, soon surrendered, or sought safety in flight. This was the first of a series of splendid victories, which were to raise him to the highest pinnacle of his youthful ambition.

Kassa directed his march in triumph to Gondar, where he established himself in his former right; but he was not long to enjoy tranquillity. Ras Ali began to fear more and more the rising power and popularity of the indomitable chief. He managed to raise a powerful army, which he placed under the command of Aligaz Faras, the bravest and most renowned of his generals, and despatched him to Dembea against Kassa. The adventurer, nothing daunted, gave battle; the result being the defeat of Ras Ali's army, Faras himself lying amongst the slain.

The Ras now saw that his own power was at stake, and determined to take the field himself. He, therefore, collected together a large army, increased by reinforcements from Oubie, prince of Tigre, who also had begun to look with suspicion on the designs of Kassa. Ali descended the heights of Debra Tabor, his capital, to Aichal, near Gorata on the lake, where he was met by the advancing troops of Kassa. A desperate encounter ensued, in which the forces of the unfortunate Ras were completely routed, and driven by their foes over the Abai or Blue River into the province of Gojam. Ras Ali escaped by flight, seeking first an asylum in the church of Mahdera Mariam, whence he fled to his kins-men the Gallas of the south. Mr. Bell, our country-man, was present on this occasion: he happened to be in the service of Ras Ali. He was not long in per-ceiving the superiority of the victor of Aichal over his former master, and on the defeat of the latter, united his fortunes and sympathies to the remarkable man whose star was now in the ascendant.

The scattered remains of Ali's army had fled to the protection of Birru Goshu, chief of Gojam, and son to the prince of the same name whom Kassa had slain on the borders of the Tsana. The victorious conqueror continued his march over the Abai to that province with the object of disposing of this last remnant of his enemies. There stands in the south of the most fertile province of Gojam an isolated mountain mass, called Djibella, which, from its inaccessibility, save by one narrow path, forms an impregnable natural fortress, and hither Birru Goshu retired at the approach of his powerful enemy. From some unknown reason, however, Goshu afterwards determined to give his enemy battle on the plains at the foot of the mountain, perhaps carried away with the hope of revenging on Kassa the death of his father. This false step involved his own defeat; for however unimpeachable his individual bravery might be, that of his army melted like wax before the very name of the terror-inspiring Kassa, and the ill-contested battle ended in the capture of Goshu himself. The province of Gojam was thus added to Kassa's dominion; and, leaving the government in the hands of one of his generals, by name Tadla Gualoo, Kassa retraced his steps to Gondar.

Thus the whole of Amhara bounded on the north by the Arab tribes of the Soudan, on the west by the Blue Nile, on the south by the country of the Gallas, and on the east by the river Tecazze, fell beneath the sway of the " kosso-vendor's son." The spirit in which he took (apparently) this good fortune is shown in the following thanksgiving, publicly uttered by him at the time:

K

"I praise thee, O God, that Thou hast manifested Thy goodness to a poor sinner like me. Whom Thou humblest is humbled, and whom Thou exaltest is exalted. Thine is the power and glory, for ever and ever." *

Arrived at Gondar, Kassa, now Ras of Amhara, sent to demand of Oubie, prince of Tigre, the tribute due to him in right of his title and established custom. This the proud ruler of Tigre indignantly refused to render, saying:

"Who art thou, ambitious usurper, that I should pay tribute to thee?"

"Thou shalt see, great Goliath," replied the indomitable chief, ever ready with one particular analogy; "for like David of old, I will soon bring down thy pride."

He accordingly prepared a large army, and marched into the mountainous country of Simyen, the frontier land of his own dominions and those of his powerful rival. Oubie had in the meantime gathered together the utmost of his force, and, crossing the Tecazze, encamped in the plain of Deraskie. Here, Kassa, after a hard day's march, arrived, and immediately ordered the attack. Inspiring new strength into his weary troops

* Stern's "Wanderings in Abyssinia."

by an eloquent harangue, in which he recapitulated their former achievements, and ridiculed the power of their opponents, he concluded with the memorable words:

"Follow me, and by the will of God to-morrow my name shall be no longer Kassa!"

For awhile the issue of the battle seemed uncertain. The Tigreans, whose numbers were not inferior to those of the Amharas, possessed also an advantage over their western countrymen in their muskets; but Oubie, having been wounded by the hand of Kassa himself, was obliged to retire from the field, and seek refuge in one of the caverns with which these mountains abound. Discovered in his hiding-place, and taken prisoner by some of Kassa's party, his capture decided the issue of the fight. The victory was followed by the taking of the fortress of Amba Hai, which contained the accumulated wealth of Oubie, consisting of a vast quantity of gold and silver ingots, 40,000 dollars, 7000 muskets, two cannons, and innumerable other articles of value.

The following day Kassa was crowned amid the acclamations of his soldiery with the title of Negoos Teodoros, King of Kings of Ethiopia.

By the battle of Deraskie, Theodore became master

of the whole of Tigre to within two days' march of the
Turkish possessions on the Red Sea; and far from stopping here, he signified his intention of dislodging these
enemies of his country from Massowah and the Abyssinian sea-board. Postponing for the present, however,
the execution of this design, after having appointed a
governor in Adowa of his newly-acquired province, he
returned to Gondar to make preparations for a descent
on the Wollo Galla territory, occupying the high mountainous regions which extend from the River Abai,
where it makes a bend on leaving Lake Tsana to the
southern kingdom of Shoa. The incursions of these
wild Gallas during the last two or three centuries had
not only dismembered from the body of the Abyssinian
nation those more southern provinces which were the
most exposed to their inroads, but had, in the country
now about to feel the wrath of Theodore, so far advanced
as to threaten completely to divide the eastern portion
of the country from the western, the territory occupied
by them running up like a vast wedge between the provinces of Amhara and Tigre. To crush the power and
check the progress of these savage Mohammedans was
Theodore's object in this present expedition. He crossed
the river Bashilo with a large army, and engaged the

troops of Adara Bille, the Galla chieftain, at Laga Gora, inflicting on them a signal defeat. Their chief was slain in the battle. He then fortified the strong position of Magdala (bitterly known to us), a mountain mass similar to Djibella in Gojam and the Guimb of Tchelga, making it at once an armoury, a treasury, and a state prison.

Theodore presently directed his attention to the independent kingdom of Shoa, then under the government of Haila Malakot, son of Sahela Selassie, to whom Harris's "Highlands of Ethiopia" has given a certain celebrity. It was not without a desperate struggle that the people of Shoa yielded to the conqueror, and their capitulation was hastened, if not caused, by the sudden death of their sovereign, while Ankobar, the capital, was being besieged. This event, no doubt, increased the awe·with which Theodore, who pretended the approval of the Almighty in his undertakings, was looked upon, both by his own people and the terrified Shoaner. These latter, their submission once given in, were favourably treated by the invader, the son of the deceased king being appointed viceroy of the kingdom, now reduced to the position of province in the newly-created Ethiopian empire. ,

In looking back over this portion of Theodore's history, it is a source of satisfaction to find that it was not marked by any of those acts of barbarous severity which have more recently made his name odious. Whether from policy, or in obedience to the better impulses of his nature, he did not allow his conquests to be marked by even the ordinary cruelties of Abyssinian warfare. Mr. Plowden, writing about this time, says of him : "He exercised the utmost clemency towards the vanquished, treating them rather as his friends than his enemies." Again, "discovering a plot against his life, the king only placed in durance those concerned, displaying in all things great clemency and generosity."

CHAPTER VIII. (*continued.*)

DEBRA TABOR.

Theodore's schemes for the regeneration of Abyssinia—Arts of peace
—Road-making—Reforms the law courts—Care of the poor—
Corrects abuses in the church—Sequestrates ecclesiastical pro-
perty—Forbids polygamy—Abolishes the slave trade—Enmity to
Mohammedanism—His reforms opposed—Blindness of the nation
—"Theodore, the scourge of the perverse"—Rebellion of Gojam
—Revolt of the Wollo Gallas—Pretention of Garad—Death of
Plowden—Death of Bell—King's grief—His awful revenge—
Account of Bell—Esteem of the king—Attachment to the English
—Rebellion of Agow Negusie—His capture and cruel death—The
empire re-united—Project against the Turks—Proposed embassy
to England and France—Arrival of Captain Cameron—King's
letter to the Queen—Rich presents.

THEODORE had thus completed the first part of his programme, namely, the re-uniting into one kingdom the
hitherto divided provinces of the empire. He returned
to the capital to inaugurate reforms in the government
of the country, and correct the crying abuses in the
administration of public justice, which resulted naturally
from a long course of anarchy. An independent and

temperate but firm ruler was wanted. He had it in view to gain, by good and paternal government, the confidence and affection of the people, and so consolidate his power in the newly-united sovereignty of Abyssinia, created by his genius. The measure was dictated by a sagacious prudence, as a preparatory step to his undertaking that scheme of conquest which had for its object the subjugation of those outlying provinces claimed by him as having been, in ancient times, included in the Ethiopian empire; together with the grand idea of attempting, at the head of his people, the rescue of the Holy Land, the land of their fathers, from the hands of the infidel.

The first edict which went forth from the royal palace was to the effect "that every one return to his lawful avocation, the merchant to his store, and the farmer to his plough."

"The proclamation was intended as a reassurance to the country, till then so distracted by civil war, that the primary aim of its ruler was imperatively directed, first, towards the establishment of peace and prosperity throughout the realm. To further this end, he gave orders to his soldiers to *purchase* their food, and in no way to harass and plunder the peasant, as had previously been done by the armed bands. The better to assist in giving his wise command a practical working character, he introduced a system of regular pay in the army. He also expressed his intention of establishing a regular standing army, armed with muskets only, and declared that he would convert swords and lances into ploughshares and reaping-hooks, and cause a plough-ox to be sold dearer than the noblest war-horse. The peasantry he sought gradually to accustom to live quietly under the village judge, and no longer to fear the terrors of a shifting military government." *

The caravan routes, closed by war, he again, to the best of his ability, made practicable, and simplified the regulations regarding commerce and customs dues. He dealt very mercilessly with the bands of highway-robbers, whose ravages, even more than the unsettled state of the country, had tended to make the roads unsafe. With the assistance of the Workmen's Mission, he commenced the construction of roads; taking Debra Tabor as centre, and connecting the capital with Gondar, Gojam, and his arsenal at Magdala; and good roads branching out in these directions were the beginning of his work. In a rich and populous country like Abys-

* Plowden's Reports.

sinia, hitherto not a single road had ever been constructed. This will show how wretchedly it had been
distracted by feuds and misgoverned by its princes;
and perhaps no greater proof could be given of the
extended grasp of the king's mind than his immediate
resolution, when power was in his hands, to have a net-
work of roads over his country.

He also sought to open up the resources of the fertile
land, by instituting explorations of the iron and coal-
fields there known to exist, and he entertained the project of sending to England and France some of his more
intelligent subjects, to learn useful arts and manufactures, as well as to induce foreign artisans to take up
their residence in his country. One of the ruling ideas
of his reign has been to attract foreign workmen, for
the chief purpose, no doubt, of getting skilled con-
structors of implements of war. His experience with
the Egyptian troops on his northern frontier had convinced him that the primitive mode of warfare of his
country would have to be superseded by the more
modern one, if he was ever to accomplish the splendid
designs of his ambition; and, as he knew that the
Turks at Massowah would never allow any great quantity of war *matériel* to pass to him through their terri-

tory, he determined to have it manufactured under his own supervision at home.

Shameful abuses in the distribution of the law, which were encouraged by the venality of the native judges, who were to a man corruptible, and held the soliciting of bribes to be no scandal, had to be reformed, and Theodore did not attack them idly. Like Moses of old, he took upon himself the decision of cases which were brought before him, making his own palace, as it were, a Court of Appeal; and it is said that the judgments thus given were often not unworthy of the wise Solomon, from whom he claims descent.

The poor he took under his especial care, and wherever he pitched his camp, he would signify his willingness to hear the complaints of the destitute, always beginning the day with this charitable work. Acting from a mixture of policy and humanity, he has sometimes, during a week's march, scattered thousands of dollars among the poor; and he would add grace to his gifts by saying, "If I do not help the poor, they will complain of me to God; I myself have been a poor man."*

Though firmly attached to the religion of his fathers,†

* Dr. Krapf's Missionary Researches.

† I give no credit to the story circulated by M. Lejean and urged by Dr. Beke, of Theodore's having once offered to compound with

his penetration, increased by the insight into monastic life received in the convent of Tchangar, had convinced him that the church as well as the state stood in need of a reformation. This community, consisting, under the Abuna, of innumerable priests and debteras, numbering nearly a quarter of the population, had, through previous royal grants and private legacies, obtained possession of one-third of the landed property of the realm, which, being farmed out to the peasantry, was to its owners a vast source of wealth, enabling them to live in idleness, and not unfrequently drunkenness and debauchery.

One of the first acts, therefore, of this Henry VIII. of Abyssinia was to sequestrate to royal purposes the whole of these demesnes, after apportioning out certain tracts surrounding each church for the support of its priests. The measure, of course, aroused the inveterate enmity of the sacerdotal caste; but the kindness ever shown by Theodore to the poor amongst them proved that he

---

Father Jacobis for the establishment of Roman Catholicism in Abyssinia. It was a rumour originated by the Jesuits, his bitterest enemies. It is quite opposed to the whole tenour of his life; nor do I believe that he would have condescended to trifle on this subject, by promising, or by affecting to promise, what he had no intention of performing.

was not conspiring against the religion of the land, and justified the act of spoliation in the eyes of the people, while the increased revenues thus obtained helped him to support his numerous soldiery, and to carry out those other measures for the improvement of the country which he had instituted, he himself living in the simplest and most unkingly manner possible.

Another of the edicts issued from the royal palace was one forbidding polygamy.

This was in reality no new law, but the enforcement of one already existing, that the apathy or bad example of previous rulers had allowed to be universally transgressed, and rendered nugatory. The immoral condition of the population sprang partly from a state of perpetual civil war; for the soldiery, the principal offenders in this respect, were often taken away for years from their homes, and feeling the inconvenience of carrying their wives and families with them, they formed fresh unions in the places where the camp took up temporary quarters. The consequences were of course detrimental to the social virtues and moral character of the people, and many families, by the husbands' desertion, were thus left totally unprovided for: much suffering and destitution were the consequences.

It was in a great measure deference to the wishes of European governments that induced Theodore to forbid the slave trade throughout his dominions. The abominable traffic was conducted mostly, though not exclusively, by his Mohammedan subjects, and the victims were principally the heathen Gallas of the south; the centre of the trade was the Basso market in Gojam, and the outlets for this peculiar kind of merchandise were Massowah and Matammah. An Abyssinian was forbidden, on the pain of death, to sell one of his own countrymen, though instances of this being done are not unfrequent, especially at Massowah; and numbers of Christian Abyssinian slaves are found at Cairo, and in general throughout the Egyptian and Turkish dominions. They, however, have for the most part been constrained into Mohammedanism; but they will often acknowledge their Christianity to an European who will not betray them; and should they regain their liberty, they shake off the creed of Islam at once.

The bitter enmity Theodore entertained towards Mohammedanism and its professors, apart from the natural antipathy of a Christian, is not to be wondered at when it is considered that to that source, above all others, was due the dismemberment and ruin of his country. The Turks in the sixteenth century had possessed themselves of the only sea-board the country possessed; the Egyptians, in their invasion of the Soudan, had overrun and annexed on the north and west some of its richest provinces, while the irruption of the Mohammedan Gallas of the south had disunited from the empire those Christian remnants which, if they have still preserved their autonomy, lie scattered abroad almost hopelessly separated from the mother-country. No wonder, therefore, that with this long accumulation of his country's wrongs to avenge, Theodore's virgin sword, drawn first on the frontiers of Kuara, should be stained with the blood of the infidel; no wonder that he should unfurl the standard of rebellion against the Galla Waisero and her son Ras Ali; no wonder at his fierce onslaught on the country of the Wollos; and no wonder—however much an enlightened Christianity might deprecate it— that another of the edicts which ushered in the new régime required peremptorily the expulsion from the country or the instant return to the bosom of the church of his apostate countrymen.

Such are some of the measures which inaugurated the accession of Theodore to the throne of Abyssinia. That they would have been carried out, and added to by others of a like nature, we may reasonably conclude, judging from the resolute and aggressive character of the monarch; but events were now about to transpire which were destined to make him put off indefinitely the execution of these schemes, and compel him to seize the sword again for the assertion of his personal rights as sovereign.

It is said of the ancient Jews that they were a rebellious and stiff-necked people, and the modern Abyssinians, who arrogate to themselves the title of Beni Israel, could not furnish a better proof of the justness of their claim to be so called than is afforded in the resemblance which they bear in this respect to the Israelites of old. Haters of all rule, they greet the uprising of those whose superiority of talent marks them out as the benefactors and saviours of their country with resistance and rebellion, while they attach themselves with ardour to any petty chief who will gratify, by a raid on their weaker neighbours, their lust for forage and plunder. Thus, for generation after generation, has their beautiful country been the scene of anarchy and bloodshed, and they have rendered themselves a prey to the aggressions of Mohammedanism, till it becomes a matter of doubt whether they will be able to maintain even their existence as a nation. Nay, their very life would long since have been crushed out, had it not been for the natural protection which their mountain wall affords them.

Under these circumstances, the only chance for Abyssinia to maintain its independence is in the whole of its provinces being united under a firm and enlightened government, and assuredly within the modern history of the country no ruler has arisen who promised better to supply this need than the present occupier of the Abyssinian throne. The blind and perverse nation, however, did not see good to recognise in him their deliverer, and his schemes for the regeneration of his country being met by revolt from all quarters of the empire, his proud and passionate nature broke through all restraints of wisdom and goodness. Seeing that he was not destined to be the saviour of his country, he determined to be the rod in the hands of God for its punishment. "I thought," he said, "that God had raised me up to be a blessing to this people, but I find I was mistaken : engrave on my cannon, ' *Theodore, the scourge of the perverse.* ' " *

I have, however, in this last paragraph rather ante-dated the terrible change in Theodore's character. It was not in view of the rebellions I am about to describe, which he soon succeeded in putting down, that Theodore fell into his unhappily permanent state of savage despair, but of those which broke out later in 1864 and 1865, and which still resist his power.

The first rebellion distracting the attention of the king from the task of supervising the domestic reforms of the country, though synchronous in time with many others, was that of the people of Gojam under Tadla Gualoo, the governor whom Theodore himself had placed over the province. The insurrection was thoroughly quelled, though Tadla Gualoo, retiring to the mountain fortress of Djibella, in the extreme south of the province, succeeded in eluding the king.

The Wollo Gallas were the next to incur his chastisement, and in this expedition an incident happened which showed that it was only because mild measures failed that he had recourse to severe ones. Having defeated and taken prisoners a number of these Gallas,

* M. Lejean's " Théodore II."

Theodore, at the instigation of the European artisans who accompanied him, generously liberated them. No sooner, however, had the enfranchised Gallas reached the outskirts of the king's camp, than with the treachery which is the characteristic of most Africans, they turned on the unsuspecting soldiers of the king, removed by distance from the main body, and commenced a wholesale slaughter. The king, on hearing of it, turned to the Europeans, and said: "You see the result of dealing gently with these people; in this instance I took your advice, for the future leave me to myself."

His absence on the campaign was the occasion of the revolt of his own brother-in-law, Garad, who seized the opportunity of investing Gondar, and putting the northern provinces under pillage. It was in withstanding this rebel that the king lost his two tried friends, Plowden and Bell. Plowden was, as we should say, British Consul for Abyssinia. I have remarked that Theodore recognised no foreigner as resident consul, for he would have no establishment of foreign consulates whatever in his country. His particular objections to it were founded on exaggerated reports of natives who have been to Jerusalem on pilgrimage, and who had represented to the king that consuls in Egypt and Syria possess powers almost equal to the governments of those countries themselves. Consuls are, it must be confessed, a fruitful source of vexation to foreign governments too frequently. Plowden was, nevertheless, much beloved by the king, and followed him in his campaigns, serving occasionally in his army.

On this occasion he was attacked in the neighbourhood of Gondar by some of Garad's party. Having but a small retinue with him at the time, he was defeated and wounded, from the effects of which he died a few days after. The king suffered intense anguish at the loss of his friend, and Maderakal told me that on first seeing the body, he was so carried away by his grief as to attempt to lay violent hands on himself. It is possible that Maderakal, however, may have rather stretched a point here as a narrator, but the king's grief was deep.

Bell, on hearing of Plowden's death, to whom he was much attached, vowed revenge on Garad. At the same time he had a singular presentiment that, in being revenged, he would forfeit his own life. The gloomy notion did not prevent him from acting. He made his will, and bade good-bye to his children and friends, and started with the king in search of Garad. They pursued the rebel into the province of Woggera, but, while passing through a wood, Garad, who had there secreted himself, rushed out, hurling a spear at the king. The latter, seeing the deadly shaft coming, had only time to stoop, when it whizzed by and went to the heart of one of his officers. In a moment Bell had drawn his pistol and fired. The ball entered his enemy's brain. Garad fell, and our countryman was thus avenged; but a brother of Garad's hurled a spear at Bell. It pierced his forehead and killed him on the spot. The king immediately, with one fell stroke, levelled Bell's murderer to the earth; and the rest, now engaging, succeeded in overcoming the enemy.

But how bitter was the anguish of the king, when he saw his other friend dead, who had fought by his side! He wept over him with excessive grief, crying, "Oh Bell, poor Bell! it was thou who savedst my life, but at the expense of thine own." Then, leaping upon the body of him who had slain his friend, he dashed his spear into the dead man's head, exclaiming: "Thou, thou wretch, hast deprived me of my best, my only friend!"

This incident shows fully the twofold character of the king: at times tender as a child, but when roused cruel as a tiger.

His revenge for the death of Bell was the mutilation

of his 1700 prisoners, whose hands and feet were chopped off, and their bodies heaped up in a pyramid and left for the hyenas to devour.

Bell, originally a naval officer in the British service, had come to Abyssinia some twenty years previously as an adventurer, and after having served some time with Ras Ali, on the defeat of that prince had entered Theodore's army, and from that time heartily espoused the cause and shared the fortunes of his royal master. The king was very grateful for these services, and conferred great honours on his new friend, making him eventually generalissimo of his army. He also bestowed on him the highly honourable though dangerous office of Lika Mankuas, a position which enjoined the person who occupied it to wear the royal habiliments during an engagement, as a blind to the enemy in distinguishing the royal person. But in addition to, and far above, all these dignities, the king made him his bosom companion and friend, consulting him when he would not trust his own nobles, and listening with the greatest condescension to his suggestions and advice; and many of the wisest measures of his reign are due to the influence our countryman had over him. No wonder, therefore, at his excessive grief over his loss, and the revenge he wrought upon those who were concerned in his death is, though shocking, the less astonishing when we bear in mind what it was that inspired his fury. The death of Bell he has always considered the greatest misfortune of his reign, and, even to this day, the slightest allusion to his friend will awaken his unfeigned manifestations of sorrow.

It is said that a missionary having once shown him a stereoscopic view of the cemetery of Melegnano, after the battle of June 1859, in which was the figure of a man weeping over the remains of his friends, slain in the battle, he burst into tears, and said: "Let me also weep, for I have lost my best friends; I am alone now." In remembrance of his two trusty friends, he conceived a strong attachment to the English nation (since, alas! utterly broken), and has been heard to say that were an Englishman to present him poison, he knowing it to be such would take it; an Eastern manner of speaking it is true, but one which it is doubtful whether he ever used in reference to any of his own or another nation. His knowledge of our national history and customs is considerable, and he might put some of our countrymen to shame by his acquaintance with Shakespeare, which he used to get Mr. Bell to translate to him, when on his campaigns the Englishman shared the royal tent. He had the habit of calling it Bell's Bible.

The lessons of the Englishmen helped the king to disconcert poor Captain Cameron during his first reception. A question of the ceremonious forms of respect due to sovereigns arose. The consul had presented the queen's letter in a sitting posture, though Captain Cameron's shortcoming was really not attributable to want of respect, but to indisposition, he being then almost prostrated with fever.

The king said to him: "In an interview with your own queen, is it customary to present a letter, seated on a chair?"

"Certainly not," said the consul, rising with an effort, and excusing himself.

But the most serious and apparently most formidable revolt was that of the province of Tigre under Agow Negusie. This pretender laid claim to the rule of that country, and from misstatements on the part of the Jesuit missionaries made to the French consul of that period, was accredited by the French Government as the rightful sovereign. Agow Negusie's portrait may be seen to this day in the photographic studios of Cairo and Alexandria as the *Roi d'Abyssinie*. It was he who bestowed on the French a small island in the Red Sea, the intended occupation of which occasioned a little anxiety to our own Government. He was supported in his rebellion by a number of disaffected chiefs, who always abound in this unhappy country, let the power be in the hands of whomsoever it may, as well as by some relations of Oubie. With the latter personalty, however, Theodore had arranged matters by a matrimonial alliance, making his daughter Iteghe or queen.

Theodore, after the defeat of Garad, hastened to put down the new insurrection, and at length came across the enemy in the valley of Tembyen, on the other side of the Tecazze. The fear inspired by his name, and the treachery of the chiefs who had espoused Negusie's party, conspired to destroy the rebel without a blow. On the day of the battle Negusie had but a handful of men left to contend with his powerful enemy, and so hopeless was the struggle, that he flew to save his life. He was recognised, however, by some peasants, and, together with his brother Tesama, taken prisoner and conducted to the presence of the king. The monarch was at first inclined to deal leniently with him. It transpired that Negusie had sought the aid of the Mohammedan Gallas; this offence was considered by the king too great to be passed over without an exhibition of condign punishment. Both brothers had the right hand and left foot cut off, and were exposed in the market-place of Adowa, with strict injunctions that not even a cup of water should be given them. Tesama died the same day, but Negusie survived three days. At his own request the spear put an end to his sufferings.

Having thus reduced a second time the whole empire under his rule, Theodore lost no time in directing his attention to the accomplishment of the second part of his programme—the bringing again within the bounds of the kingdom those outlying provinces which the Turks on the coast, and Egypt on the north and west, had conquered from its previous rulers. But before pro-. ceeding to this he deemed it wise to obtain the recognition of the two European nations of England and France, and proposed to send ambassadors to both countries to seek their friendship and to justify to them the course he was about to take. Just at this time an incident happened that seemed to promise material aid to him in his plans. It was no less than the arrival at his court of Captain Cameron, the newly-appointed British Consul for Abyssinia. Accompanying the consul, and acting in the capacity of his secretary, was a

M. Bardel, a Frenchman. To these two gentlemen his Majesty entrusted letters to the governments of their respective countries, the tenor of which, as stated by the king to M. Lejean afterwards, was to ascertain the willingness of the French emperor and of our own queen to receive and guarantee a safe passage through Egypt of King Theodore's ambassadors. The following is a copy of the letter to Queen Victoria:

"In the name of the Father, of the Son, and of the Holy Ghost, one God in Trinity.

"The chosen by God, King of Kings, Theodoros of Ethiopia, to her Majesty, Victoria, Queen of England.

"I hope your Majesty is in good health. By the power of God I am well.

"My fathers the emperors having forgotten our Creator, He handed over their kingdom to the Gallas and Turks. But God created me, lifted me out of the dust, and restored this empire to my rule. He endowed me with power, and enabled me to stand in the place of my fathers. By His power I drove away the Gallas. As for the Turks, I have told them to leave the land of my ancestors. They refuse. I am now going to wrestle with them.

"Mr. Plowden, and my late Grand Chamberlain, the Englishman Bell, used to tell me that there is a great

Christian queen, who loves all Christians. When they said to me this, ' We are able to make you known to her and establish friendship between you,' then in those times I was very glad. I gave them my love, thinking that I had found your Majesty's good-will. All men are subject to death, and my enemies, thinking to injure me, killed these my friends. But by the power of God I have exterminated those enemies, not leaving one alive, though they were of my own family, that I may get, by the power of God, your friendship.

"I was prevented by the Turks occupying the sea-coast from sending you an embassy when I was in difficulty. Consul Cameron arrived with a letter and presents of friendship. By the power of God I was very glad hearing of your welfare, and being assured of your amity. I have received your presents, and thank you much.

"I fear that if I send ambassadors with presents of amity by Consul Cameron they may be arrested by the Turks.

" And now I wish that you may arrange for the safe passage of my ambassadors everywhere on the road.

"I wish to have an answer to this letter by Consul Cameron, and that he may conduct my embassy to England.

" See how the Islam oppress the Christian."

The letter to Napoleon, which we have reason to believe was similarly worded, M. Bardel bore himself to Paris, while that to our queen was despatched to Aden, to be thence forwarded to its destination. Pending the arrival of an answer, Captain Cameron proposed to himself a journey through the Egyptian territory to the north, with the object of inquiring into the slave-traffic of those parts, and also of examining the country, with a view to its adaptability for the growth of the cotton plant. In the meanwhile, the king gave orders to the Armenian silversmiths of Adowa for the preparation of some rich presents to be sent with the embassy. These were to consist, as far as our queen was concerned, of fourteen horses richly caparisoned with saddles and harness worked with gold and silver filagree work, silver shields, spears, swords, armlets, anklets, &c. The horses were to be the finest his kingdom produced, and were to be sent with the idea of promoting the Abyssinian breed in England, not improbably from a previous suggestion of Mr. Bell's.

As this brings me to the period of my visit, I shall now continue the narrative of my own experiences.

CHAPTER IX.

DEBRA TABOR.

THE king's stay at Debra Tabor was short, his object
having principally been a visit to the Iteghe or queen.
After three or four days he returned to the camp at
Wofferghef, not, however, before he had given orders
for the proper accommodation of the French consul.
A rich silk marquee, a present of the Pasha of Egypt
to his Majesty, was pitched on a low eminence close to
Gaffat by the side of a pretty little mountain torrent
which runs round the hill of Gaffat to connect its
waters with the River Reb. A smaller tent was also

pitched alongside for the accommodation of his servants, and Azage Garat, governor of Debra Tabor, was
ordered to supply the consul with a sheep daily, an ox
every week, and bread, honey-wine, &c., *ad libitum.*
The king gave orders for me to remain for the time
being with Mr. Waldmaier, though he had promised,
if I was desirous of staying in his country, to have a
house erected for me. Mr. Waldmaier had several
houses on his premises, being those originally occupied
by Mr. Bell, his father-in-law, but he was about this time
engaged in building a rather pretentious stone edifice,
à l'Allemand, in memory of the fatherland. It was
double-fronted, and had a story above, so that it could
boast of four rooms, an unheard-of luxury in Abyssinia.
Pending its completion, however, he occupied one of
the huts, giving up another to me for my sleeping
apartment. He lived mostly in the Abyssinian style,
occasionally varying it with an European dinner. The
rest of the residents will now and then do the same, if
merely for the sake of keeping the knives and forks
from rusting.

The time spent at Gaffat was occupied by several
little excursions in the neighbourhood, among others
one to the valley of the Reb, the lower course of whose

stream we had passed on our way from Genda. It has its source in the mountains to the east, and after making a large curve to the northwards, resumes a westerly direction and disembogues in Lake Tsana.

From the hill of Gaffat we took a north-easterly direction over an undulating plain with scanty flora, and through which winds on its way to the river the little beck before-mentioned, which supplies Gaffat with water. Before us rose the mountain monarch of Melza, rising up in a peak which probably attains the height of 14,000 feet, and whose lower buttresses protrude into the northern side of the Reb valley. On the road we passed through the enclosure of a native church, consisting of a pretty cypress-wood, and a few hundred yards thence reached the edge of the deep ravine, through which the river holds its difficult course. The sides of the ravine are clothed in the richest foliage,—the harbour of monkeys and a great variety of birds,—while below the river's banks are again concealed in thick umbrageous trees, or occasionally disentangled from these accessories, the Reb flows on in a silver stream through a narrow strip of meadow land, whose bright emerald green contrasts well with the sombre mass of foliage by which it is on all sides surrounded. An opening in the trees on the opposite side of the river disclosed now and then vertically-ribbed basaltic rocks, which form perpendicular walls of 100 feet or more in depth.

We had brought our guns with us in search of game, but an occasional gazelle, too wary for us, or a monkey or two not worth powder, being all we saw, we were glad to discontinue our laborious barefoot climbing along the sides of the ravine and descend into the valley, where, in a kind of bower formed by parasite plants curved over the lower branches of a tree, we laid down to rest and enjoy our *dolce far niente*. We had brought food with us, and we commenced cutting and slashing away at it, as if it had been the wild boars we had come in search of. A box of sardines, of whose existence in Abyssinia we had not dared to dream, dropped down in our midst, as though descended from heaven, though our more immediate benefactor was M. Lagarde, the French doctor.

On another occasion we made a visit to the summit of Gunna, a vast mountain mass to the east, which is frequently seen capped with snow. The consul and myself had resolved to make this excursion, so one day we had our mules saddled, and, attended by some

M

domestics to show the way, we started. We had six
hours of a beautiful country to pass through before
reaching the foot of the mountain, and here again we
saw the Reb, dwindled now to a small stream, for it
has its source amongst the heights above. We had
only about 4000 feet to ascend, for Gaffat itself is
nearly 11,000 feet above the sea, the two heights together making Mount Gunna about 15,000 feet. Half-
way up we stopped at a small village at the house
of Mr. Bell's widow and her family, or rather the
family of which she forms a part, consisting of her
mother and grandmother, and no end of brothers and
sisters. She was about this time also made a grandmother herself; Mrs. Waldmaier, her daughter by Bell,
had just been delivered of her first child, so that there
were five generations of them all alive. This goes
far to prove the longevity of these mountain people;
indeed, I have heard of some of the Simyen moun-
taineers living to the advanced age of 120 and even
140 years.

Another remarkable thing is, that these people I
saw, who have lived for generations on these mountains, possess a much lighter complexion than other
Abyssinians, a proof that the low humid valleys of

tropical countries have more to do in producing the black hue of the people than any fancied difference of primal origin. The next morning, after a fearful night, in which we were almost rolled out of bed by colossal fleas, we renewed the ascent. It was accomplished on mule-back, which was rendered easier from the nature of the mountain, this being of a long ridge-like shape, and possessing spurs or offshoots on either side, on the upper edge of one of which our animals found no difficulty in making progress. On attaining one of the lower summits we saw by the thick clouds now gathered around us that we were doomed to disappointment as far as an extensive view was concerned, so we did not think it worth our while to climb the remaining 200 feet. The view from the highest point is said to extend to a great distance in each direction, embracing the country of the Wollo Galla, through which runs the Bashilo to its junction with the Abai, the mountains of Gojam, the borders of Lake Tsana, including Mount Tabor, and extending to the north by Mount Melza, until a distant view of the Simyen heights is obtained. The cold was intense; I could scarcely hold the bridle of my mule. Dismounting for a short time to admit of M. Lejean's taking a topographical survey of the adjacent valleys, which a break in the clouds would occasionally disclose, we could with difficulty endure the keen atmosphere, and had to practise gymnastics for warmth. Our descent, therefore, was speedily decided on, and by a forced march we reached the same day our quarters at Gaffat.

During our stay an order came from the king for the erection of a capacious stone workshop for the use of the European artisans, and the mushroom-like celerity with which this building sprang up was amazing; for in a despotic country like Abyssinia, the will of the monarch can command any amount of labour, and all other private interests must yield to it. A thousand Jews and Galla slaves were at once sent to the spot. Many of the latter were chained together, either on account of some misdemeanour or to prevent them from absconding. These servile Gallas are mostly taken in battle, or are descendants of tribes long settled in the country. As amongst the Abyssinians one finds also amongst the Gallas a great variety of type, varying from the copper colour to the jet black; from the thin lip and aquiline nose of the Arab to the prognathous physiognomy of the negro. They differ also in language, though these differences appear to be mostly dialectic. I should place their capabilities on a par, if not above those of the Habeshi, considering the advantages the latter possess in their knowledge of the Christian religion. Mr. Waldmaier has several Gallas entrusted to him by the king for instruction in the mechanical arts, and one of them has risen to be his chief workman. This man executes carpentering work with a skill and neatness to be surpassed by few Europeans working under the same conditions; nor is his intelligence confined to mechanical labours. He displays a corresponding vivacity of mind in literary occupations; he is a remarkably good reader and writer of Amharic; and on one occasion he constructed for M. Lejean an excellent map of his country, Kulloo, some 500 miles to the south, whence he was extracted in childhood and taken into slavery.

The Jews are numerous round Lake Tsana, and are either builders or blacksmiths. They resemble in appearance the other Abyssinians; perhaps they are a little blacker in skin. They are called Falashas or exiles; and are much despised by the Christian portion of the community, who accuse many of them—indeed all blacksmiths—of being *boudas*, or sorcerers.

The first duty of these labourers was to clear away the large stones, which here, as throughout the whole of Abyssinia, cover the face of the ground. This done, and the space which the building would occupy marked out with a simple kind of pickaxe, the foundation was dug, and the work of building commenced. Lime is scarce in the country, so mud is used for mortar; and the unhewn stones, which are so plentiful, are arranged with great neatness. The building was 100 feet long by thirty feet in breadth, the latter being also the height of the wall, which was three feet thick. The whole was completed in about ten days. Here were to be accommodated: Mr. Waldmaier as carpenter, Mr. Saalsmüller as blacksmith, and M. Bourgaud as gunsmith; but the building was mainly intended to serve as a foundry for cannon and mortars, in which all the Europeans are engaged.*

The Abyssinians themselves were beginning to profit by intercourse with these artisans. While I was at Debra Tabor they produced a small mortar which, considering the manner in which it was made, was a marvel. The metal was melted in some thirty crucibles, on fires

* I see, from recent letters of the captives, that the king has just had this building destroyed. Why, it is difficult to say.

in the ground, blown by hand-bellows of the most primitive description—consisting of a leather bag, the mouth of which is opened on being drawn up for the receipt of air, and closed again when the air is to be driven by pressure through the clay tube conducting to the fire. As is natural, every encouragement is given by the king to his people in their endeavours to perfect themselves in the manufacture of these implements, for he is fully aware that this is the best way for him to secure his independence of other nations; and with this idea he also contemplated sending natives to England and France for the purpose of learning useful trades.

I had the satisfaction of seeing in Gaffat a case of *Bouda*. This term is given to some peculiar phenomena of mental abstraction, which the natives explain as being possessed by the devil. The case I am about to mention happened to a female in the service of one of the Europeans. Her symptoms began in a kind of fainting fit, in which the fingers were clenched in the palms of the hands, the eyes glazed, the nostrils distended, and the whole body stiff and inflexible. Afterwards she commenced a hideous laugh in imitation of the hyena, and began running about on all fours; she was then seized by the bystanders, and a bouda doctor having been called, this individual began questioning her as to the person who had possessed her with this hyena devil. She said he was a man living in Gooderoo, south of Abyssinia, and also told how long the spirit would be in possession, and what was required to expel him. Great care must be taken of persons thus afflicted, as cases of this kind sometimes end in death. All their demands for dress, food, trifles of any sort, must be strictly attended to. In the height of the frenzy they will sometimes carry out the idea of their hyena identity to such an extent as to attack any animal that may happen to be in the way. One woman fancied she would like a little donkey-flesh; so to gratify her strange taste she seized hold by her teeth to the hinder part of one which happened to be near. Off went the astonished beast, at a pace that nothing in the form of persuasion will lead him to adopt for the gratification of man. Off, too, clinging tight with her teeth to his haunches, went the frenzied girl. Only force would induce her to forego the tender morsel.

They have several cures for this strange attack; but the never-failing one is a mixture of some obscene filth, which is concealed in some part of the house, whereupon the woman is said to go directly, on all-fours, to where it is and swallow it. This would seem incredible, but thousands of corroborative facts, known to Abyssinian residents, put it beyond a doubt.

As I have observed above, the power of possessing persons with the devil is attributed mostly to Jewish blacksmiths; and women and children are terrified when they meet, in a solitary place, a blacksmith who is a Jew. These sorcerers are also said to be endued with the power of changing the shape of the object of their incantations. Mansfield Parkyns relates an amusing incident of this nature, which is said to have occurred in Adowa. An old lady, who had a numerous family of grown-up children, was one day missed from her home, and search having been instituted all over the town, could nowhere be found. This inexplicable absence very much puzzled her sons, and at last forced on them the conclusion that she had been cruelly brought under the influence of some wizard's incantations; but weeks passed over and no clue was found to the explication of the mystery. It happened, however, that one of the sons, who was in the habit of sitting in the porch of his house, had frequently noticed on market days an old Jew riding by upon an ass, and that this ass, whenever it came near the house, turned its face in that direction and commenced braying with all its might. This circumstance, though often occurring, did not at first excite his suspicion; but at last the startling truth flashed upon his mind, and with a loud Eureka! he proclaimed to his assembled brothers that that ass was his mother. The ass and its rider were seized, and the latter compelled to confess, that by his supernatural powers he had transformed the old woman into this useful animal. He then asserted his willingness, if they would not further molest him, to bring back their mother to her original human form. The proposition was agreed to, and he at once commenced the task of restoring her. The head, the body, the arms, and one leg had all gradually assumed the human shape, and the remaining leg was slowly progressing towards the same happy consummation, when the son, who had found out his mother's identity, could no longer restrain his anger against the miscreant Jew, but with a blow of his spear killed him on the spot. Alas! no sooner was the Jew dead than the transformation ceased, and the poor old lady was left to carry about with her, through the remainder of her life, the hoof-remembrance of her former condition. I asked

Maderakal, who is a native of Adowa, if he had heard the story? "Oh, yes!" he exclaimed, "the 'Children of the Ass' remain to this day!"

Pending the absence of the king, Azage Garad, the Governor of Debra Tabor, invited all the Europeans to a feast at his residence on the mountain. This is close to the site of the king's new palace, about two miles from Gaffat, and 500 feet higher up the mountain. So we saddled our mules, and in holiday attire proceeded to accept the invitation of the great man. The Chrischona brethren are in good relation with the Azage, notwithstanding that it was he who imprisoned their servants at the command of the king. He also is in great favour with his Majesty, and holds one of the highest posts in the kingdom—the charge of the royal hareem being committed to him. He is a tall, well-made, light-complexioned, and handsome man. Our mules being left outside in charge of the domestics, we entered the capacious hut prepared for our reception; but happening by accident to look aside before going in, I saw the ox being driven into the inclosure which was to serve for breakfast. "We shall have it fresh," I thought. The ground within the hut was strewn with carpets, upon which were placed large wicker baskets covered over with scarlet cloth. After we had been seated, chatting some time, the Azage entered, and, as usual, we all rose and inquired, "How he had passed the time since we had last met?"

The Abyssinian form of greeting has a copious phraseology. On meeting a person after some length of time they will say, "How have you passed the time since I saw you last?" And if, on parting, a corresponding period is likely to elapse before another meeting, they say, "May you pass the time well till I see you again." In the early morning they say, "How have you spent the night?"—and then, on leaving, "May you spend the middle of the day happily." In the afternoon the greeting is, "How have you spent the noon?"—the good-bye being, "May you pass the evening pleasantly;"—and so on throughout the day. The invariable reply to these inquiries is *"Egziair yemasgen,"* "May God bless you!" Towards an equal or a superior you must use the second person plural, but you are allowed to *thou* your servant. Speaking of a great person you must use the third person plural, *ersatchou*—they, them.

The entrance of the Azage was the signal for the circulation of the hydromel or *tedge*. This was kept in large *gumbos* or stone jars with narrow necks, covered with a piece of cotton-cloth, through which to drain it, so that the leaves of the *gesho,* a plant used in the making of the wine, may not pass through. From these gumbos it is poured into narrow-necked Venetian flasks called *barillyè,* these being preferred to glasses, as the dust and flies are thus excluded in a great measure. Notwithstanding this advantage pertaining to the barillyè, in a great man's house it is not uncommon to see coloured glass tumblers, which, being scarce and expensive, are considered articles of luxury. The servant, after presenting the tedge, always holds out the hollow of his hand, which the receiver fills with wine, and sees the servant drink before he will taste himself—it is the provision against poison. The Abyssinians also present and receive everything with both hands, even if it be a pinch of snuff; they have a peculiar fondness for snuff, taking it into the mouth in preference to the nose.

The signal was now given to gather round, and we all huddled together round the baskets. The covers were removed and disclosed large piles of teff-cakes, about a foot and a half in diameter and half an inch thick. The surface of each was covered with large holes like a sponge, which in their soft springy nature they did not a little resemble. Iron stands were brought and placed alongside each basket, ready to receive a seething-dish or pot of minced mutton, almost lost in a thick red-pepper butter-gravy. The servant, having carefully washed his hands, now takes half of a teff-cake, and using it as a cockney often does a cabbage-leaf that serves as a support for peas-pudding, scoops up an allotment of the mutton and thick gravy and places it on the summit of the bread pile. We tuck up our sleeves and fall to, breaking off pieces of bread and rolling up a mutton-pill inside, which we swallow as well as we can, using the tedge to wash it down. If there is not enough pepper, which by-the-bye was seldom the case as far as we were concerned, you can dip it into a pile of Cayenne, which is placed on some convenient part of the bread-plate.

The time occupied in this first course is considered ample to prepare the ox outside for presentation to you as a second course; strips of his reeking carcase, about a yard long, are brought in by some half-dozen servants. The Abyssinians like their meat fresh, and, unlike some British gourmands who await both the death and *resurrection* of their venison, they scarcely wait for the last expiring breath of the animal before they cut off the quivering flesh and bring it thus to table. Knives are now passed round, except to those who are already provided with swords, and we each cut off what might be called a *bif tick au naturel*; if you wish to be *à la mode* you must not lay your piece of meat down and commence cutting it into morsels, but placing a corner of it into your mouth, with an upward motion of the knife (taking care of your nose) you cut off successive mouthfuls. The remainder of the meat in the servants' hands, having now got cold, is semi-broiled over a good fire in the hut; it serves for the last course; puddings, sweets, and dessert are unknown here. Your table napkin is one of the undermost cakes, on which you wipe your hands; it is considered rude to suck them, as amongst the Arabs. The napkin amongst the rest is received with thanks by the servants, and duly devoured.

CHAPTER X.

WOFFERGHEF.

Set out for the king's camp—Town and mountain of Tabor—Garden
of Africa—Arrival in camp—Wofferghef—An Abyssinian army—
Military discipline—Departure of king for Gojam—My farthest
south—Tadla Gualoo—Failure of king's expedition—Probable
cause — Imprisonment of French consul — My preparation for
leaving.

A SHORT while after the king's return to his camp at
Wofferghef, an order came from his Majesty for the
attendance of the whole of the Europeans. Wofferghef,
which I believe means the Valley of Birds, is about
fifty miles south of Debra Tabor, and within a short
distance of the Abai.

As soon as we had made the requisite preparations in
the way of tents, provisions, &c., we commenced the
journey. Passing down the steep sides of the hill on
which Gaffat is situated, covered with thistles, thorn
bushes, wild mint, and a few odd castor-oil plants, we
crossed the little beck and began our ascent to Debra

Tabor, as we had to pass that village on the road. The plain extends to the foot of Mount Jesus, the highest point of the Tabor range. Crossing it, we continued our way up a rugged path, and quickly attained the summit of the mountain. The town is situated a little below the highest point, and consists of a number of scattered huts, probably containing a population of 5000. Close by is the Church of Jesus, or as we should say Christ's Church, one of the largest in Abyssinia; it possesses a good bell, instead of the usual kettle-drums. It is situated in a plantation of magnificent forest trees, the kosso, the cypress, and the juniper amongst others. From this spot a fine view is obtained of the surrounding country, embracing the pyramidal cone of Melza, the high ridge of Gunna, and to the south the ranges of hills on either side the Abai. Lake Tsana is excluded by an offshoot of the mountain itself.

A very steep descent conducts into the valley through which runs the River Foggera, on its way to join the Tsana lake; and on the grassy banks of this stream, beneath the shade of some beautiful trees, we stayed to take our noon-day rest. We afterwards continued our journey over two or three ridges of low hills

to Mahdera Mariam, an important village on the summit
of a high plateau. We encamped at the foot of the
table-land, pitching our tents in close proximity to that
of the queen, who was also journeying to the camp.

Once on this march, I was gratified by a sight of
the fair Toronetch, Iteghe or Sultana to the Abyssinian
monarch; but as she was muffled up to the eyes with
a superabundance of rich garments, my view was confined to the two brilliant orbs, which, if report be
correct, have often returned the withering fire of her
royal husband's. Theodore gives little love to the
beautiful daughter of Oubie, but he is proud of being
the possessor of the fairest and most accomplished of
Abyssinian princesses. Nor has she herself much affection for the man who dethroned her father, and still
holds him prisoner; and, as her pride is as great as
his, their wills often clash, and frequent differences and
separations are the result. The king has also a certain
number of favourites, who form a kind of hareem, but
he has only taken to these since the death of his first
wife, Tsoobedge, to whom he was deeply attached and
devotedly constant. She alone of all his mistresses
gave him any real love, and she consequently had a
great influence over him for good. Had Tsoobedge and

his English friends, Bell and Plowden, lived, Theodore might possibly have been a different man, and his present complication with the British nation would never have occurred.

The next day we crossed another stream, a feeder of the Foggera, draining a country of the richest and most luxuriant description. As the king was about to make an expedition into Gojam to subdue the rebel Tadla Gualoo he had ordered supplies from all the neighbourhood, so that the whole length of the road was occupied by thousands of men and women, horses, mules and donkeys, carrying provisions, &c. The last mortar which had been made was also now transported to the camp, suspended from the middle of two long poles, the ends of which passed over the shoulders of several men.

In the afternoon of the third day, after passing through a beautiful park-like country, we arrived in camp. We entered somewhat in martial order, Mr. Moritz undertaking to keep us in rank, which as a soldier he was well capable of doing. We were about a dozen, all mounted upon mules with gay ornaments, the harness in many instances covered with gold and silver work, which, with gay-coloured silk and velvet tunics,

and the crimson-bordered *shamaa*, made us look rather
imposing. As I have before said, I had myself adopted
the Abyssinian dress, and even went so far as to go
barefooted, and that for four months. Though Abyssinia
is not the smoothest of countries to commence the
practice in, I must say that I found it preferable to
wearing shoes.

The camp presented a remarkably fine sight. The
whole length of a broad valley, some five or six miles
in extent, was covered with thousands of black and
white tents, over which, on a slight eminence in the
centre, presided the three coloured silk marquees of the
king. Innumerable cattle, mules, and horses grazed
around, and groups of soldiers, with their bristling
spears, stood round the fires watching the progress of
culinary operations, while the pale blue smoke slowly
ascended in the undisturbed atmosphere, wreathing
itself round the summits of the low hills which bounded
the valley. The appearance of the camp at night was
even more impressive than during the day, the innumerable watch-fires lighting up each little scene in
front of the nearer tents; while the fires extending into
the distance, diminished to mere specks of light, put
one in mind of the night view of some vast city. As

most of our party had tents with them, a place was allotted to us where they were to be pitched; our arrival was notified to the king, whereupon each party was furnished immediately with a cow and five sheep.

The next morning we were invited to breakfast in one of the king's tents, but we had no interview with his Majesty. The king afterwards sent to express his intention of proceeding at once to Gojam, and to inform us that he required the company of all the Europeans, Waldmaier, Bourgaud, and myself excepted. It was left to the option of the French consul to accompany them or not. He preferred the former. One marquee was to be left for the accommodation of the queen, and this was surrounded in an incredibly short space of time with a thick palisade formed of the branches of trees. A part of the army sufficient for her protection was also left under the command of Azage Garad. The rest, preceded by the king, the French consul, and the Europeans, departed on the following morning.

The king's army possibly consisted of some 50,000 warriors, but the number of camp-followers is often double that of the army itself, which of course adds much to the unmanageableness of the whole. Indeed there is little or no system in Abyssinian warfare. It consists in rushing pell-mell upon the foe, hurling the spear, which is their principal arm, and picking up and re-hurling the spent darts of the enemy. The musket, which is mostly in the hands of the Tigrean soldiers, is even less effective than the spear, and the amount of powder and shot wasted must be enormous. The sword is seldom brought into requisition (unless it be in eating *brundo* or raw flesh), as arm to arm combat is unfrequent; and I actually saw one individual, though certainly this was not in the camp, who had allowed the blade so to rust in the scabbard that it was quite impossible to draw it. These swords are in the shape of scimitars, curled up into a semicircle, resembling a dog's tail, and are always getting entangled with the dress or the trappings of the horses. The sheaths are not strong, and one frequently sees the point of the weapon peeping out at the end, though in some cases this is prevented by a large brass knob, or even a lady's thimble, stuck on the end. The best hilts are made of the horns of the rhinoceros, and ornamented with silver. The spears are about six feet long, the length of the head being one foot, and the breadth two inches in the broadest part. The butt has a piece of iron twisted round it to prevent vacillation in the aim. The shields, made of hippopotamus hide, are a foot and a half in diameter and about half an inch thick. They are sometimes ornamented with silver, and the tail of a leopard or lion is affixed to the boss. The guns are mostly flint. Cartridges are kept in short pieces of reed fastened together so as to form a girdle. The dress of the soldier does not differ from that of the people, except that some officers are allowed to wear gay-coloured tunics. The war-dance is very wild and uncouth, consisting of leaping off the ground and whirling the spear, sword, and gun over the head, accompanied by a song, at the end of every verse of which a peculiar *ching-ching* sound is heard, uttered by the voice, but resembling that of cymbals.

Not many pieces of cannon were then in the country, and they were seldom used as field-pieces, artillery practice being unknown to the military tactics of Abyssinia.* The king himself is much in favour of adopting European discipline in the army, and once made an attempt by placing 1000 men in the hands of Mr. Bell, his English

* I have not been able to ascertain whether cannon-founding has been going on to any great extent since my visit; but if the European and native artisans at Gaffat have been well employed during the last four years, the king must now possess a goodly number of pieces of v ious kinds (cannons, mortars, &c.).

general, with the object of having them trained; but as in the native Egyptian army, in the time of Mohammed Ali, the measure produced so much dissatisfaction, approaching to rebellion amongst the soldiers, that he was compelled at last to desist.

I was somewhat disappointed myself in not being able to go to Gojam, but dared not call in question the commands of the king. Wofferghef, my farthest advance south, is about four hours from the Abai, as the Blue Nile is here called on leaving Lake Tsana. I should very much have liked to have seen the old stream again, so full of associations connected with the previous two years; but I had endured many disappointments before and had become seasoned to them, so that I took this as it came.

The king's expedition into Gojam was not so successful as he had anticipated. His enemy, Tadla Gualoo, convinced that an open engagement would end in his destruction, had taken the wise precaution to retire to the impregnable fortress of Djibella, which he regularly keeps provisioned for ten years. The king, with his shrewd foresight, saw that the bombardment of the mountain was the most likely method for dislodging the rebel, and for this purpose he had commanded the

construction of mortars at the hands of the Chrischona
workmen, and had retained them at his disposal to work
them. For some reason or other, when within a short
distance of the mountain, he suddenly relinquished his
purpose, and, after sacking and pillaging a few villages
on the route, commanded a retreat. I was anxious to
ascertain the motive for this sudden return, and made
inquiry about it, but I could learn but little in explanation. It was said that disease had broken out in the
army, that a conspiracy had been discovered amongst
his chiefs, and that the stores had failed ; but I believe
the most potent reason of all was the sudden appearance
of 8000 Turkish soldiers at Matammah on his frontiers.
I have before mentioned that, in consequence of the
letter sent by Theodore to Said Pasha, the Egyptian
viceroy had deemed it advisable to despatch Musa
Pasha with 10,000 men into the Soudan. The bulk of
these, after remaining a short time at Khartoum, had
pushed on to Gellabat, with the alleged purpose of
punishing a tribe within the Turkish frontier who had
refused payment of the tribute. It was said that the
army had no orders to proceed to Matammah, and after
a few days they were recalled by Musa to Gedárif ; but
it is not unlikely that the whole expedition was a move-

ment on the part of the Turks with the object of intimidating King Theodore. A Mohammedan chief in Dembea was prompt to take advantage of their proximity to desert and join the Turks, and this so vexed the king that on his return from Gojam he sent his soldiers to pillage the whole province for their having suffered the traitor to escape. The return of the Turks to Gedárif, however, set the possibility of invasion at rest for the time being; and, turning his attention again to the consolidation of his power in his own country, Theodore gave orders to the Europeans for the construction of some yet bigger mortars. He also wished them to direct their attention to the founding of cannon, so that, when the rainy season should be over, he might, by a well-managed *coup de main*, annihilate the rebel chief at Gojam. Four years have elapsed since the period I treat of, and Theodore's task remains still unaccomplished. Tadla Gualoo still waves the rebel flag from the walls of his mountain fortress.

The French consul's resolution to accompany the king was somewhat unfortunate for himself, as after events proved. M. Lejean, before leaving Gaffat, had despatched a servant to the coast with letters for his Government, but on his arrival at Gojam he heard that this servant was detained at Gondar. He therefore asked the king's permission to leave himself immediately, as it was highly important the despatches should be forwarded. The king replied that as they were now in the enemy's country it was impossible for him to go alone, as he would be probably taken prisoner by some of Tadla Gualoo's party, and then he (the king) would be responsible to the French Government for suffering him, in those circumstances, to proceed. He said, moreover, it would require a very large escort to ensure safety, and this he could not spare. The consul declared his willingness to take all responsibility on himself; but the king still refused his consent. On two subsequent occasions M. Lejean repeated his attempt to gain the king's permission. On the third the king was so vexed at the continued application that he dismissed the consul angrily from his presence and ordered him to be put in chains. The following day, however, on M. Lejean's promising that he would neither seek to escape nor renew the question of his leaving, the chains were taken off. I can testify that from this time until the day of my departure in June he was very well treated by Theodore, who had a hut erected for him at Debra Tabor, and supplied munificently all his wants. He was detained, however, until the arrival of a M. Bardel, whom the emperor had despatched previously to France; on whose return, in the following September, he was liberated, and departed for h is own country.

On the king's return to Wofferghef I took the opportunity of sending to ask permission to leave. Three or four days after I received a letter from his Majesty, in which, after the usual inquiry how I had passed the time, &c., he gave me full permission to depart either by the Matammah frontier or by way of Massowah. Of course I preferred the latter, and a Tigrean soldier about to proceed to Adowa was appointed as my guide as far as that place. I wished to go by way of Gondar, desiring to see the capital; but as the soldier bore a special message from the king to Mr. Schimper at Adowa, he was obliged to go the nearest way. My disappointment in not being able to see Gondar was, however, somewhat compensated for by the prospect of passing through a country out of the beaten track of most European travellers.

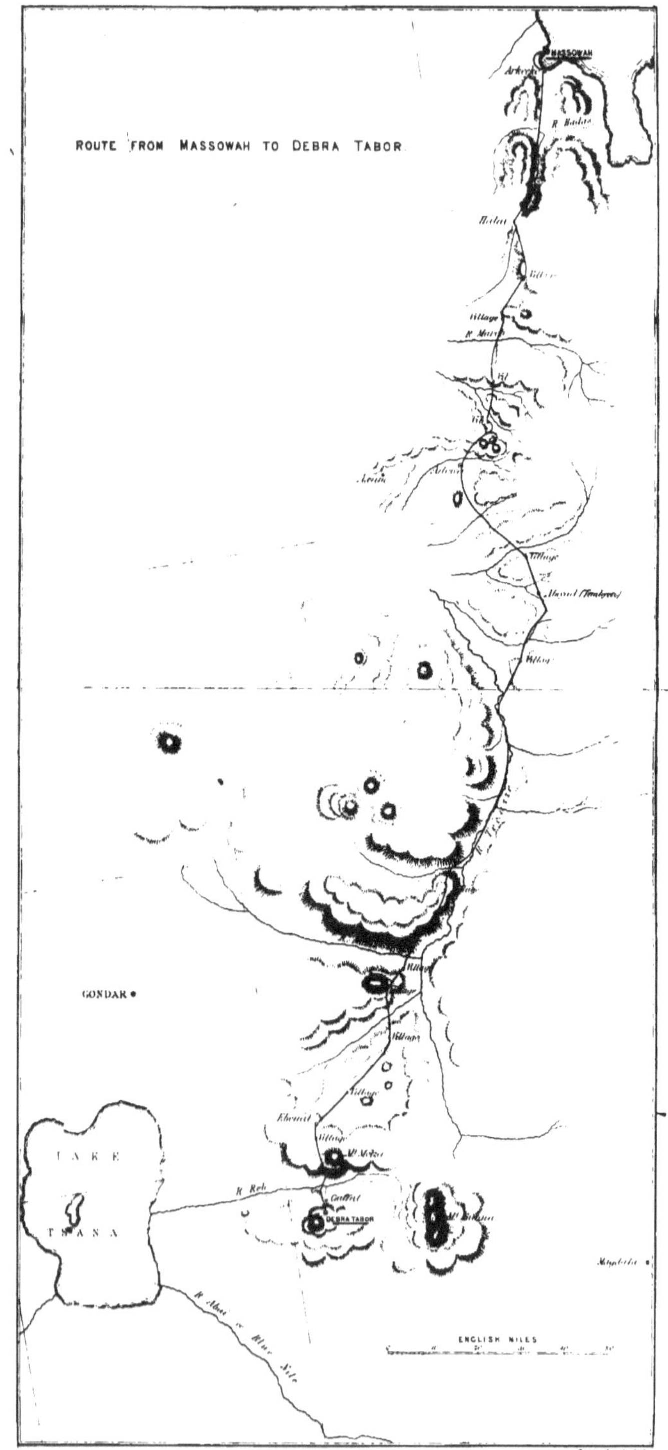

ROUTE FROM MASSOWAH TO DEBRA TABOR.
MASSOWAH
GONDAR
LAKE
TSANA
DEBRA TABOR
ENGLISH MILES

CHAPTER XI.

DEBRA TABOR TO ADOWA.

Departure from Debra Tabor — River Reb and Mount Melza —
Ebenat — Abyssinian inhospitality — Farewell to my donkey —
Province of Bellesa—The Agows—Geology—Paroquets and mon-
keys—River Minna—Flora of Abyssinia—Snowy mountains of
Simyen—Native customs—River Tecazze—Enter Tigre—Town of
Tembyen—Nature of the country—Anecdote of a donkey's tail—
Arrival at Adowa—The second capital of Habesh—Abyssinian
greed—Axum and its remains—Live ox eating.

It was about the middle of April when I left the
European colony of Gaffat, where my stay had been
prolonged to about three months. Our party consisted of myself, Worku, a servant I had engaged ut
Wofferghef, two servants of M. Bourgaud, who were
proceeding to Massowah to fetch some goods lately
arrived from France, and also two servants of Mr.
Kiensle, on their way to Adowa, to return with the
daughter of Mr. Schimper, about to be united in happy
wedlock to their master. The Tigrean soldier, who

acted as guide, bore also a letter from the king to Mr.
Schimper, requesting him, as a dutiful subject, to deliver up his daughter to his (the king's) " child" Kiensle.
Azage Garad, governor of Debra Tabor, had given orders
for our party to be supplied at every village we should
rest at for the night, with a sheep, bread, beer, &c., in
the name of *Teodoros yemoot*.

The province of Begemder (Land of Sheep), in which
Debra Tabor is situated, is bounded on the north-east
by the River Reb; and, continuing in a northern direction, down the steep slope of a spur of the Tabor range,
we at noon reached the banks of this stream. As it was
the end of the dry season, and the rains had not yet
commenced, the river was easily fordable. The scenery
in the Reb valley is very beautiful,—rock and wood
being thrown together in every variety of attractive-
ness; Mount Melza always presiding, like a protecting
giant, over the beauty of the landscape at his feet.
Crossing the Reb, we commenced the ascent of a similar
steep to the one we had just descended, up a corresponding offshoot of the Melza, and towards evening
reached an extensive plain, a little below that mountain's highest point, in which is situated the large village
of Ebenat.

The demand for food and lodging brought the grey-beards of the village out to hold a long palaver about our right to the articles in question, but the "Teodoros yemoot" had its due effect, for the proximity to Debra Tabor was too great to allow of any demurring to the Azage's command. In villages more removed from the seat of power, the order was not unfrequently set at naught, which did not seem to show much for the loyalty of the people, or for their hospitality. On one or two occasions they refused even bread, and we were obliged to go to bed without supper, and proceed next day without breakfast. Such a thing never happened to me amongst the Arabs, notwithstanding the difference of religion between us; and here, as elsewhere, I found that the Mohammedan Abyssinians were far more hospitable, as well as more industrious, than their Christian neighbours. I am fully aware that it must be very hard for such extensive demands for hospitality to be made on poor people like the occupiers of these villages; and on a frequented route like that from Gondar to Adowa, I should scarcely blame the people if they refused to grant them; but on the road I was travelling, demands of this nature were scarcely ever made upon them, and their refusal to comply with the king's order was both rebellious and uncharitable. The continued unpleasantness which was the result induced me afterwards to pay for what I managed to obtain.

At Ebenat I was obliged to bid a long farewell to my donkey, it being unitedly predicted that he would surely succumb under the fatigues of the journey, and he was left here to be sent on to Gaffat when opportunity should occur. His load consisted merely of a few books, and one or two other small articles; it was not this, therefore, which prevented him from proceeding, but the rough nature of the country. I had hoped that during the three months of his absolute idleness at Gaffat he would have picked up sufficient strength for the journey, especially as he had abundance of thistle fodder, to say nothing of a regular feed of corn, but he appeared to put it into a bad skin, for he still looked rather emaciated in comparison with the Abyssinian asses around him. This want of good appearance, however, did not prevent him from comporting himself like a true Mussulman amongst the Nazarene kafer donkeys with whom he was obliged to hold intercourse. He always maintained his slow stately walk; not even a stick would make him alter that. I was very sorry to part with my old friend, who had been of such small service to me.

On leaving Ebenat we skirted the sides of a cone-like hill, which marks the northern termination of the irregular plain, and thence began an abrupt descent into a low flat valley of black alluvial soil, covered with thorny trees, the nearest distance being occupied by high flat-topped mountains of transition rock. The country is thinly inhabited, and there were few signs of cultivation. We were now in the province of Bellesa.

Traversing the length of this valley, we again began to ascend, reaching on the fourth evening a rugged tract, in the province of Lasta, occupied by the Agows, a tribe supposed to be a relic of the older inhabitants of the country. Their language differs both from the Amharic and the Tigrinya. They are scattered about all over Abyssinia, and are most abundant to the south of Lake Tsana, near the sources of the Blue River The Bogos, a people to the north-east of the Abyssinian frontier, are said to be of the same extraction.

Our road was excessively rough, there being scarcely the semblance of a path. The whole of this part of the country seems to be of secondary formation, consisting of a fine sandstone, which has been exposed to immense heat, and is very hard, and of a dark-brown colour.

The perfect horizontality of the mountain plateaus, which meet the eye on every hand, would seem to imply the non-existence of subterranean action, and yet it is difficult to account for the innumerable shattered fragments of rock and stone which cover the surface of the valleys. The undermining of the lower portions of these table-lands by the flow of water, and the consequent giving way of the upper parts, would possibly account for it. In some parts, however, the extreme regularity in which these blocks of stone appear to have been deposited, extending in a marked line along the sides of the valley, the larger stones nowhere mixed with the smaller ones, would seem to point to the agency of glaciers, though such must be comparatively unknown at present. What is remarkable is, that these stones are not in the least water-worn, but have all very angular surfaces. The only specimens I saw of water-worn boulders consisted of a red granite, like the syenite of Upper Egypt, and they were only found in one spot in the province of Bellesa.

Notwithstanding the rocky nature of the country it abounds in trees of every description, which are the retreat of innumerable paroquets and monkeys, whose chatter and jabbering are almost deafening. These monkeys express no fear, seldom retreating at your approach, but sitting in the branches of the trees over your head, grinning at you with their exposed teeth, as they coolly finish eating their nuts or berries. I believe they are of the common African ape species. Their colour is a greyish-brown, and they are about two feet in height.

The fifth day we arrived at noon on the banks of the River Minna, a broad mountain stream, whose sides are adorned with fine tamarind and sycamore-fig trees. Nothing increases the pleasure of travelling in Abyssinia so much as being sure always of obtaining a cool shady tree for your noon-day rest. The whole country abounds in trees capable of affording this. The sycamore, cypress, tamarind, juniper, kolquol, acacia, and *kosso*, may be mentioned amongst others, the latter peculiar to this country. Its fruit is the famous cure for the tapeworm, so universal a complaint of Abyssinia.

The River Minna flows into the Tecazze, the main tributary of the Atbara, which enters the Nile in Berber. We passed the beds of many other mountain torrents, but they were all dry, though each bore signs of being powerful streams in the season of rains, which made me easily credit the assertion of my servants that the country was totally impassable at those times. I saw here in heaps of black earth, thirty or forty feet high, skirting the sides of the mountains, the tokens of extensive lakes or backwaters, that are gathered in vast sheets by the want of an outlet for the streams descending from the hills, or from the draining of the swollen rivers into isolated valleys.

My sight was now delighted by frequeut views of the summits of the Simyen mountains, thickly covered with snow. As this was the month of April, one of the hottest, I can easily believe that some of these mountains are never free, but are within the region of perpetual winter. They are the highest in Abyssinia, attaining an elevation of 15,000 ft. in Aboo Yared, the loftiest peak. Our route took us along the sides of these mountains, where the air was cool and refreshing compared with the stifling heat of the lower river valleys.

We were now in the province of Simyen. This district is thinly peopled, and it was not often we got our demand for a sheep supplied. The greediness of the men who were with me was very great, as they would often eat the whole sheep over night, instead of saving a part for the succeeding day. Worku deserved a little praise for the care with which he looked after my interest, seizing the portion of the animal he knew I liked best, and seeing that I had my supper before the rest were allowed to taste. When strangers were in the hut, or I was eating out of doors, a *shamaa* was put up as a screen, so that no evil eye should look upon his master feeding. At the slaughter of every sheep the paunch and liver of the animal are cut up raw into very small pieces, and the contents of the gall-bladder squeezed over the whole, so as to form what the Abyssinians consider a very tasty dish. The mess was sometimes handed round to me in a wooden bowl, but notwithstanding my apprenticeship at *brundo* eating, the raw inside of a sheep with these "appurtenances" was really more than I could stomach. The above practice is also common, I am told, amongst the neighbouring Arabs; and I have seen an Arab eat the intestines after they have been cooked over a fire.

We reached the Tecazze the day after leaving the Minna, which it scarcely surpassed in volume of water. This induces me to think the latter its main tributary, as supplied from the snows of Simyen it is worthy of being. As it was the end of the dry season one could the more easily judge of the relative importance of each feeder, for during the rains other tributaries assume an importance not due to them, depending on the locality of the breaking thunderstorm, and not on a perennial source. The water was very low, not exceeding three feet in the deepest, which was a great advantage to us, as having to travel two days along its bed, from the winding nature of its course, we were necessitated to cross some twenty times each day. The breadth of the river bed has an average of some fifty yards, but the stream itself at this time seldom exceeded twenty. It is for the most part locked in by high walls of transition rock, quite flat at the top, which is about 100 feet from the river's bed. There is no sign in the inclination of strata of this being a chasm through which the stream has its flow; but the river appears to have cut its own way, which it certainly must have taken some ages to have performed. Along the tops of these rocks large troops of monkeys were occasionally to be seen, marching in great regularity behind a leader, and sometimes descending to the river's bank to drink. Vast quantities of driftwood lay scattered over the dry portion of the river's bed; I saw frequently whole trees which had been torn up by their roots. With these at night we made large fires to keep away the hyenas and jackals infesting these parts. Not a house had we seen down the whole length of the stream, so we were necessitated to sleep out. My servant used to cut some of the long grass found near at hand, and with this make me an excellent bed on the shingle.

The Tecazze is the boundary line between Amhara and Tigre, the western and eastern portions of Abyssinia, and we were now entering the latter, leaving behind us the high mountains of Simyen. On quitting the Tecazze we passed through a district of slaty formation, whose line of cleavage was at right angles to the road, and presented a rugged surface very unpleasant for our mules. Thence we began to descend into a low narrow valley, through which the Gevha, a small mountain torrent, has its course. A little beyond this we entered the village of Tembyen, situated in a beautiful grassy glen, at the foot of some rugged mountains, and at the bottom of which runs a small stream of pure water. This village is Mohammedan, and has an occasional market. We happened to arrive on a market-day. About 2000 people were assembled in the market-place, and there was great hubbub and some confusion. This is the last place where the salt of Amhara is taken as money. The nearer one gets to the coast where are the salt mines, of course the less is the value of the mineral; and in Tigre, cotton cloth takes its place as a medium of exchange. Along our previous road we had met some hundreds of asses and mules laden with these bars of salt, probably proceeding from the Danakil country to Amhara.

Though we had still three days' journey to make, we could see from Tembyen the high mountains of Adowa, whose fantastic peaks are a prominent object all the country round. They appeared to be situated in an extensive plain, but my experience of the previous route led me to expect that beneath these seeming plains lay concealed deep tortuous valleys. The conjecture proved to be right. The road also, being little frequented, was excessively rugged, so that I was often compelled to dismount for the sake of my mule. Occasionally we had to pass along the steep sides of deep ravines, where one false step would have hurled us to the bottom; and here I saw the value of the mule in such countries as Abyssinia; no other animal is so safe and sure-footed.

In this neighbourhood one of M. Bourgaud's mules died on the road, upon which his servant cut off a piece of the tail to convince his master that there had been no humbug. I well remember the first occasion of my seeing this strange custom. One day I was sitting with M. Lejean in the tent, when one of his servants came in, and with a good deal of demonstration and talk, which from ignorance of the language we could not comprehend, presented the consul with a bloody trophy of some kind. Supposing, naturally, that it belonged to some wild animal we examined it with the greatest attention and curiosity. Of course, each ventured an opinion, but nothing definite was decided, and the servant with his Amharic could not help us in our solution of the difficulty. We puzzled ourselves sometime longer, until at last the truth in all its ludicrousness burst upon the mind of the consul, as with a hearty laugh at our ignorance of comparative anatomy he exclaimed, "*Mais ! c'est la queue de mon baudet !*"

In the morning of the last day we passed the curious rock of Damo, rising to a height of 500 or 600 feet, one side being quite perpendicular. This is the first of a chain of high hills which surround Adowa; and thence, ascending a little, we passed round a mountain bluff, and now beheld the second capital of Abyssinia, with its large pretty-looking churches, nestling in the valley below. Adowa, with a population of about 10,000, is the principal town of Tigre, situated by a small stream which enters the Tecazze some hundred miles to the south. It is considered healthy, for though situated in a valley, it has an elevation of about 4000 feet above the sea-level. There is no great attraction in the place itself, except that the houses are a little more comfortable and solidly constructed than in most other villages, some boasting of two stories; but the town is not without its interest in having been the scene of many an event which has affected the condition of all Abyssinia. No one can relate its modern history better than Mr. Schimper, a German botanist, who has resided here for twenty-six years, and the only regret is that he, the best informed of all the Europeans who have visited the country, has not yet published anything on the subject. He has, however, made some fine botanical collections, which have been despatched to Germany, France, and England. He several times invited me to his house during my stay, and I found him of most agreeable company. I had also the pleasure of being introduced to his daughter, the bride of Mr. Kiensle. She is a half-caste, the daughter of an Abyssinian lady, but she has much more of her father's complexion than of her mother's; and I found that her education had not been neglected. She could speak German as well as the languages of Abyssinia. When she heard that she was going to be married, the young maiden covered her face and ran away.

My sojourn in Adowa was prolonged to a fortnight, as I had a slight attack of dysentery, which weakened me very much. During this time I stayed at the house of Maderakal's mother, as he had requested me, allowing the two servants of M. Bourgaud to stay also with me to keep Worku company. Mr. Kiensle's servants stayed, of course, with Mr. Schimper, and the soldier who had acted as guide was dismissed with a suitable reward. The three remaining ones thought that they would live well as long as they remained in this land of plenty; and, I having kept the strings of my purse pretty loose, in ten days they had demolished three or four sheep, besides vast quantities of pease - pudding (*shimbra*), bread, beer, and honey-wine. I then began to think it advisable to retrench, and get away as soon as possible, notwithstanding my illness.

While at Adowa, I paid a visit to the ancient city
of Axum, situated half a day to the west. On the
road I passed a village entirely deserted. Its inhabitants had all been called out by a conscription to
join Theodore in his wars. The remains of the ancient
city of Axum consist of a number of variously-shaped
obelisks, most of them lying prostrate, but one or two
still standing, beneath which are large square blocks
of stone, having runnels cut into them as if for the
reception of some liquid. Mr. Schimper maintains that
they were originally used as altars, on which the aton-
ing victim was offered up. The principal obelisk which
still remains erect is sixty feet high, and, unlike the
Egyptian obelisk, is not square-sided, but broader than
it is thick; neither does it rise to a point, but is
rounded off at the top. It has no hieroglyphics, but
has some ornamental work on the face; the lower part,
just above the altar, is made to represent a door, with
the wooden lock exactly of the description now used
in Egyptian and Arabian towns. What makes this
remarkable is, that such kind of locks are quite unknown in Abyssinia at present. The granite from
which these huge monoliths have been cut is found
in the neighbouring hills. A tablet containing some

Hamyaritic inscriptions is found in a private house
of the town. I did not see it. In the midst of these
obelisks stands a large daroo or sycamore tree, whose
spreading branches embrace several of them within
their extensive shade.

Axum also boasts of possessing the principal church
of Abyssinia, built of an oblong square form wholly
of stone. In it is said to be concealed the true ark,
which was stolen from the Jews and brought hither.
The church enclosures are a place of refuge for all
criminal and political offenders, no man daring to seize
or expel them thence. I heard, however, that King
Theodore had once infringed this ecclesiastical law, and
boldly arrested some of his enemies here. My servant
maintained that both the church and obelisks were
originally erected by the devil, who resided here for
some time. The modern town of Axum is large, almost
as much so as Adowa. It is built round about the
church and obelisks, and it is quite possible that some
of the houses still conceal precious remains of anti-
quity. Axum is situated at the extremity of a large
plain between some low hills by which it is shielded
on the north.

It was between Axum and Adowa that Bruce witnessed the case of live-ox eating, which so affected his fame at home. Now, in a country where I have seen eaten and often partaken of flesh warm and quivering from the ox, actually moving in the hand, —where it is a custom also to eat the raw paunch and liver, with the gall-juice of the goat, and where a native told me it was common for shepherds to cut a sheep's tail while alive and suck the fat out, filling the wound with salt for another occasion, — I can readily believe to have taken place what Bruce described, especially as he never insisted on its being a practice, but only an exceptional case.

CHAPTER XII.

ADOWA TO MASSOWAH.

Leave Adowa—Anarchy of Abyssinia—Geology of the country—
Evidences of volcanic action—River Mareb—Variety of tempera-
tures—Halai—Vermin—Jesuit missionaries—The Shoho tribes—
Descent of the Taranta—An albino—Quarrel with the guide—
Digging for water—Novel method of procuring fire—Bread-baking
—Arrival at Arkeeko—First view of the Red Sea—News of Cap-
tain Cameron—Mkulloo—Mr. Kerens—Massowah.

Towards the end of May I left for Massowah. Mr.
Schimper, accompanied by his daughter, Mr. Kiensle's
servants, and also those of M. Bourgaud (who had been
met at Adowa by another party bringing forward that
gentleman's baggage) left two days before myself for
Debra Tabor. At Adowa I had engaged another
servant to carry my few goods, who, with Worku and a
guide, were now all the retinue I could boast. My
gaily-caparisoned mule, however, the mark of the
dignity of chief, still constituted me a great man in a
small way.

There are two routes from Adowa to the coast. I should have preferred traversing the one least frequented through Hamaseyn; but from the unsettled nature of the country it was considered unsafe; so that I was obliged to take that through Halai. We not unfrequently heard of rebel chiefs who occupied some of the roads, for some parts of the country were merely in nominal subjection to Theodore. It will be a matter of great difficulty to unite all the disconnected particles, of which the political state of this country consists, into one kingdom or empire, accustomed as the people have been for ages to recognise in a king nothing but the name of majesty.

The country through which I passed was similar in its nature to the previous part of my journey. Valleys within valleys, mountains upon mountains, constitute the physical features of Abyssinia. This is admirably shown on the road between Adowa and the eastern frontiers. A few peaks, of a height varying between 8000 and 10,000 feet, form the highest parts of the country, and seem to be a relic of a former condition of the earth. These appear also to correspond with the high masses of Gunna, Debra Tabor, Melza and Simyen, and probably also with those of the Wollo

Galla, Gojam, and other parts. The detritus of these, worn down by continued tropical rains, and, perhaps, by glaciers and avalanches, appears, in process of time, to have formed a vast table-land once covering a greater part of the country. The flat-topped mountains round Wekhni, the Guimb, Magdala, the high plateaus of Bellesa, the hill on which Mahdera Mariam is situated, that in Gojam, which Tadla Gualoo has made his retreat, but more especially the portions of Abyssinia I was now traversing, are remains of this second condition of the country. But this in its turn has been abraded by the continued action of rain and atmospheric influence, till its even stratified surface has become indented with deep valleys, and these latter it is which constitute perhaps the greater part of the present Abyssinia. The whole of the country has a very consolidated appearance. The almost total absence of inclined strata would seem to imply that the earthquakes, which are said to be frequently felt, must be feeble in power, not exerting any great influence in changing the configuration of the country. A small volcano exists at Ait on the sea-coast, and Maderakal told me that some few years since the ground of one of the plains of Tigre was seen to open and emit huge

P

quantities of smoke.   Coupled with the fact that earth-
quake shocks are most frequent near the coast, and that
the aiguille mountains surrounding Adowa are formed
of a rock which shows signs of having been forced up in
a molten state, this would perhaps betoken the greater
proximity of the central fires in the eastern than in the
western portions of the country.

In two days after our departure from Adowa we
crossed the river Mareb. Some travellers maintain
that it is lost in the sands before reaching the Atbara;
but Mr. Schimper, I believe, reckons that he has seen
the junction of the two rivers. The discrepancy may
be accounted for by the supposition that in times of
extraordinary rains it may succeed in overcoming the
sandy obstruction to which it usually succumbs. It is
certainly very difficult to fancy that so much water can
thus be lost; but it is a well-known fact that many
African streams terminate in this abrupt way. The
Mareb would appear to have a very low level. Soon
after passing it we had to make a steep ascent up the
rugged sides of a mountain, which brought us again on
to the cooler highlands. We continued upon the
pleasant upper levels until we reached Halai. It is
remarkable how in Abyssinia the vegetation changes

with the increase of level, and Mr. Schimper has constructed a map of the mountains round Adowa with all
their heights estimated, not from thermometric observa-
tions of boiling point, but according to the known habitat
of various plants.   The puff-ball tree and some peculiar
grasses so common in Upper Egypt and the Soudan
are also found here, but only in the low river valleys,
where the temperature also corresponds to those countries ; whereas the kolquol tree, the aloe, the wild rose,
and honeysuckle are never found but on the higher levels.

Halai is situated in a concavity, which the Abyssinian
table-land here takes like a mighty wave before it
crests into the heights of Taranta Mountain, thence
to descend in an abrupt steep of 8000 or 9000 feet to.
the sea-shore.   It is in the midst of a well-wooded
country, and the whole neighbourhood is under rich
cultivation.   The climate is so cool that I could sit out
in the sunshine and still feel chilly.   The town is built
partly of conical huts, and partly of square ones.   The
square huts are pretty general in Eastern Abyssinia, and
are constructed mostly of the wood of the kolquol, which
is white like deal, but much more soft and fibrous.   The
result of so uncleanly a people as the Abyssinians
using this soft wood, is, that it harbours immense

numbers of bugs, one of the more prominent curses of the country.   I was led to the house of the chief man of the village, a certain Aito Georgis, who lodged me until I should be able to proceed.   What with a renewal of ague and want of sleep at nights, caused by the above-mentioned vermin, who had "smelt the bloo of an Englishman," and came in showers from the roof, as well as from the interstices of the wooden alga on which I was lying, my reminiscences of this stay of two or three days are far from being pleasant.

I was visited here by some native Romish priests, who had crosses and medals on their necks.   They are the fruits of the Jesuit mission, commenced in Abyssinia by Father Jacobis in 1840.   The worthy father established himself at Gondar, and there continued, proselytising until he excited the animosity of the Abuna, who influenced the king to have him expelled. The king was willing enough to do it, for the Jesuits all along had opposed Theodore's claims, he having defeated and deprived of power Ras Oubie, who was their friend and patron.   It is said that at first Father Jacobis refused to leave when ordered, but afterwards, finding his life in danger, fled in disguise.   On his arrival at the frontier he still continued his missionary work, and also his political intrigues; but death put an end to both soon afterwards. The Jesuits gave every support in their power to Agow Negusie. Such a course of conduct has necessarily tended only the more to keep them out of the country as long as the present king is in power.

I was here advised to dispose of my mule, as I was informed (which information was false, by the by) that no one would purchase it at the coast. Aito Georgis promised that if I would sell it to him he would lend me another to take me to Massowah; and the bargain was struck, mule and saddle going for six dollars. I now engaged a guide to conduct me through the territory of the Shohos, who occupy the country between the Abyssinian frontier and the coast. These are a tribe of the Danakil nation, and resembling in their savage nature their neighbours the Somalis and Gallas. The man whom I engaged appeared to be a chief; he was entitled to wear a coil of brass wire round his spear. The ordinary pay for a guide is half a dollar; but I being a Frank was expected to give more, and after a little bickering the agreement was finally made for a dollar down, and half a dollar in addition on arrival at Massowah.

The descent of the Taranta is extremely difficult, and so steep that it was in vain to attempt riding down. I was fain to make the downward passage barefooted. Assuredly, I never saw anything to be compared to this. I should think we made a sheer descent, little short of perpendicular, of about 8000 feet; and, as we were hemmed in on all sides by mountains, it appeared like going down into the very bowels of the earth. After descending thus more than three hours, we arrived into a rocky wady with a stream of pure water coursing through it. Following the stream for about five miles we arrived at a place called Tubbo, where we halted for the night. We had but completed a quarter of the way, but next morning my Shoho guide wished to return, and demanded a dollar. I refused positively, saying that I had engaged him to go to Massowah, and unless he went I should give him nothing more. He still insisted, saying that the muleteer who was also a Shoho would act as guide. Now I knew that I should have to pay the muleteer for his services apart from the guide, and although aware that I could not prevent the other from returning, I was determined he should get nothing more from me for his impudence. My refusal to comply enraged him, and he said that now I was in his country he would keep me until I paid. "Well," said I, arranging a seat underneath a tree, and pulling out a volume of the 'Popular Educator,' "we will see who gets tired soonest." It was a beautiful spot where we were encamped, the wady here opening a little so as to afford a sufficient level for the growth of a number of good shady trees. Although there were no signs of human habitation in the neighbourhood, it was a station of the wandering Shohos who bring grain from the coast; the mountains afford no land capable of cultivation. The grain is brought mostly on the backs of cattle; throughout the land of the Shohos cattle are made into beasts of burden. An occasional camel would also get up as far as here, the first which I had seen for a long while; mountainous highlands are not adapted for this animal. We had a hard job to keep the mule in check when it first saw a camel; it evinced real fear in the presence of this curious long-legged creature.

The Shohos, many of whom I saw here, differ somewhat in appearance from the Abyssinians; they are tall and lanky, having the features, especially the nose, strongly marked. They wear the hair in a large bush, similar to the Arab tribes of the Soudan, where it is jokingly called a parasol. A wooden skewer, sometimes two-pronged, but generally single, is stuck into it, which is used as a comb in dressing it, or as a long pole to stir up the game which find a retreat in this thick wood. The Shoho language differs both from those of Abyssinia and from the Arabic. They are not numerous, being estimated by Rüppel at only 300; while the Danakil nation, of which they form a part, though occupying a large extent of country, cannot exceed a few thousand. They are Mohammedans, the most bigoted of the bigoted, at the same time that they know absolutely nothing. At Tubbo I saw a Shoho albino with white hair and pink flesh, looking just like a boiled European. Whether he was born so, or whether this colour may be attributed to some cutaneous disease, I do not know. At Khartoum and other places I frequently saw natives having large patches of pink in the midst of the black of their bodies, but never could hear any satisfactory explanation of the cause for it.

The sun had now passed the meridian, and with its commencing decline the Shohos, who had sought here an hour or two's rest from its heat, departed on their way, and we were left alone; I still remained reclining beneath the tree, studying my lesson in Natural Philosophy. The muleteer had gone on to the mountains seeking fodder for the mule, and my Abyssinian servants who, like cowards, had all the morning knelt blubbering before me and the Shoho, in order to induce us to proceed, now came to me to propose a very summary way of disposing of the latter individual. This " son of a dog " (by which polite cognomen I had not ceased to address him since early morning) was lying on the sand close by fast asleep, and my servants now proposed that I should go and cut his throat, and then we could bury him in the sand. I was somewhat startled at this cool proposal, and scarcely thought they could mean what they said, but they seemed earnest enough about it.

We remained there the whole of that day and succeeding night; and the next morning the Shoho came and demanded the dollar again. Of course I refused, and said that if he remained there till Doomsday he should not get it. My servants still begged that I would give it, but I remained firm. One of them then demanded his pay and wished to return. I felt it nothing but right to comply in his case, and so let him go. Worku was now at his wit's end, and taking off his shamaa and long girdle, with tears streaming down his face, knelt down before the Shoho and begged he would take these instead of the money, and let us proceed. Vexed beyond measure at the abject entreaties he addressed to the rascal, I jumped up and snatched them from the Shoho's hands. He, thinking I was about to strike him, raised his club above his head, and I might in a moment more perhaps have had my pate cracked, but that the muleteer and some others seized hold of him. He made as if he wanted to dash at me ; whether he meant it or not I cannot say. I was quite unarmed, having previously sold my gun, and he had spear, sword, club, and shield, so I felt it a quite unequal contest and kept prudently quiet. But if I had been in possession of fire-arms I might possibly have shot him with as little compunction as if he had been a dog. The truth was, the absence of my gun, and nothing else, occasioned me all this trouble, for had I possessed fire-arms he would never have dared to detain me.

About noon a party of Shohos, coming from the direction of Massowah, arrived, and having heard the whole affair, one of them, who spoke a little Arabic, came and talked to me, advising me to yield; but when he saw my obstinacy, he then proposed to go back to Massowah with me himself. This I agreed to, saying, that having paid for a guide I would have one or pay nothing more. He then went to the Shoho chief, and although they did not see me observe it, I saw him pass a dollar to the villain. I was vexed to think that he got anything, but I determined the other should not lose by it if he behaved himself well.

We were now, after a delay of a day and a half, on the road again, continuing along the bed of the mountain torrent, the perpendicular heights on each side still compelling us to follow its winding course. The stream though in some places so deep as to afford a bath (a luxury that I indulged in), is in others quite lost in the sand, flowing out again a little farther on, where the rocky nature of the ground prevents it from thus being swallowed up. As the wady widens, however, the sands increase, until at last the stream is entirely lost; and at the spot where we rested at sunset we were obliged to dig four or five feet for water, and then only were we rewarded by a draught of thick muddy fluid. My Shoho had a very novel way of making a fire as well as of baking bread. The former feat was accomplished by the aid of two dry sticks, one held on the ground firmly by the knee, while the second, being placed in an upright position in a small hole drilled in the former, is made to revolve by being rubbed between

the hands, the friction serving to produce the necessary
heat to set fire to the wood.   When the fire was kindled
a few large round pebbles were placed in the centre to
get well heated; the flour and water has meanwhile
been kneaded into the consistency of dough capable of
taking the shape of a cup.   One of the hot pebbles is
placed inside the cup and the dough rolled over it, so
as to form a ball.   In this shape it is placed in the ashes
of the fire and well turned until the outside is baked;
the heated stone serves to bake the inside.   Another
primitive mode of baking I have witnessed, and one
equally novel to me.   A hole is made in the sand, a
number of good-sized pebbles are placed in the hole,
a fire is kindled on the top; when this has burnt down
the red-hot embers are removed on one side and the
liquid dough poured over the hot pebbles, the hot ashes
are drawn over the upper surface, and the whole covered
with earth; in a quarter of an hour all is removed, and
discloses a large loaf or cake inside.   Sometimes a whole
sheep will be cooked in the same way.   While these
culinary operations were going on I took a stroll in the
neighbourhood, and about a hundred yards off came to
a kind of grotto formed by a number of stalactites suspended from the overhanging rock.   All along the

Tecazze I had noticed these petrifactions wherever the water had succeeded in penetrating the upper strata, but nowhere had I seen anything to compare to this.

At the proposition of the Shoho we determined to travel by night to make up for lost time; and after leaving the mountains we traversed an undulating plain with scanty vegetation and void of water. After a couple of hours' sleep in the early morning we again went on, and, tired and thirsty, arrived a little before noon at the town of Arkeeko.

It was with inexpressible delight I saw again the bright blue waves of the sea—and that the Red Sea. This was the first time I had ever seen it, and its placid surface seemed to produce in my own breast a corresponding calm and quiet; the turbulent passions which had lately held possession there were now hushed to rest. I discharged the Shoho at this place, giving him twenty-five piastres. I gave him the dollar first, wishing to see whether he would complain, but on the contrary he thanked me and seemed contented, which somewhat surprised me, considering that I had seen him give a dollar to the chief. I then gave him five piastres more, determined that he should not have his trouble for nothing.

Arkeeko is fortified and garrisoned by the Turks; and, strange though it may appear, I seemed to welcome Mohammedanism again as a pleasant exchange for the worse Christianity of Habesh. Perhaps this might be attributed to my better acquaintance with Moslem customs, as well as my possessing in Arabic a surer means of communication with my fellow-men, than what my slight smattering of Amharic had lately afforded me. Entering an Arab café I squatted down amongst them, and over a cup of coffee treated them to the latest news about the great Kassa, Sultan of Habesh, whom they appear a little to respect, more to fear, but most to hate. I learnt definitely that the British consul had gone to Kassela, and so my hopes of seeing him were frustrated.

Towards evening I rode on to Mkulloo, where the private house of the consul is, and was there received by a young gentleman of the name of Kerens, the first Englishman I had seen since leaving Khartoum; as also by Mertcha, an Abyssinian who had been educated at Bombay, and was, in the consul's absence, discharging the duties of the consulate. From these I got more detailed information concerning Captain Cameron's movements. He had left with the intention of proceeding through the territory of the Turks north of Abyssinia, and re-entering that country by way of Matammah, whence, after an interview with the king, he intended proceeding to England by the Nile route, as his health had not been good and necessitated his relinquishment of the consulate. I was also told that an English gunboat with government despatches was every day expected to arrive at Massowah, and that Mr. Kerens was only awaiting these before proceeding to rejoin Captain Cameron in Abyssinia. I of course thought it would be a fine opportunity of getting on to Aden, but I was doomed to be disappointed here also.

I discharged Worku, my servant, who had come with me all the way from Wofferghef, giving him, in addition to his wages, an extra dollar or two and a *shamaa*. He availed himself of the chance of returning with some of his people who had brought hides down to the coast for sale. A great deal of these are exported from here, as they are remarkably cheap in the upper country, the animal itself only valuing from 15s. to 20s. The Abyssinian, however puffed up with pride he may be in his own country, is a very tame creature at the coast, and often suffers great ill-treatment at the hands of the Moslems. One was murdered about ten miles off during my stay. They are not called Nasara here, as Christians in Egypt are, but Makada or Kustân (Christian). The term Makada is also applied to the country, originating I think from Makada, the queen of Sheba, who visited Solomon. The general term for an Abyssinian, however, is Habeshi. The people of the coast are of Ethiopian race, and speak a language called Tigrinyika, which is allied to the Tigrinya or language of Tigre; and these two, with the Amharic, form the modern representatives of the old Ethiopic.

In company with Mr. Kerens and Mertcha I made frequent visits to Massowah, where the consulate is situated. The place is about four miles from Mkulloo, and occupies a small coral island about a furlong from the mainland. It has a good harbour, where ships of the largest burden may safely anchor. The streets of the town are very narrow, as a protection against the heat, which I here found more oppressive than in any place I had hitherto been at. They are formed of two-storied houses. The residences of the governor, the consulate, &c., are of a superior description, stuccoed and whitewashed as in Cairo. The market is not large but is plentiful, containing the produce and manufactures of Europe, Asia, and Africa. A good trade is carried on with India, which is in the hands of the Banians, whose sallow faces, surmounted by their peculiar high turbans, I had several opportunities of beholding here. The principal trade of Massowah, however, is with the opposite coast, especially the ports of Jidda and Hodeida, whence a great number of small Arab craft cross with Arabian produce, principally corn, dates, and fruit, taking in exchange ghee or liquid butter, hides, honey, coffee, &c. It was in one of these boats that after a stay of about a week, during which time I had looked out in vain for an opportunity of going to Aden direct, I took a passage over to Hodeida. I was informed that thence it would not be difficult to get another vessel for Aden.

CHAPTER XIII.

MASSOWAH TO ADEN.

Departure from Massowah—Arab navigation—Appearance of Abyssinian coast — Arrival at Hodeida — Contrast of Japhetic and Shemitic races—Life in Hodeida—*Kéf*—Europeanized Turks—Ard el-Yemen—Curious auction sale—Coffee and pipe—Leave Hodeida—Touch at Mocha—"Real Mocha coffee"—Unpleasant adventure—Bab el-Mandeb—Arab timidity—Arrival at Aden.

"*Insh' allah nesafer ellaileh.*" "Please God we shall sail to-night," said the Nakhuda of the Arab vessel in reply to a question I had made; but it pleased God to let us leave on the morrow, for which I was deeply thankful, as the time stated generally requires a multiple of ten with these people, and not two, as in this instance. It was rather a sorry boat to trust oneself to for venturing 200 miles into the open sea; it did not exceed in size the ordinary Nile boat, and was rigged with the same large triangular sail which appears to be the acme of the Arab art of navigation. The Nakhuda or captain was an African Arab, but the crew were

Suahili negroes and Somalis. We were freighted with *semneh* (liquid butter), contained in large earthen jars. There were a good many passengers, mostly Turkish soldiers changing quarters from Arkeeko to Yemen, who paid nothing for their passage, the authorities compelling the transport of soldiers upon the owners of these small vessels. Among the other passengers were a young Syrian and his wife proceeding to Bombay. The rest called him a Christian, but I fancied myself he was a Jew. He had been on a visit to King Theodore with an object which he kept very close in the present company, but which I was informed while at Mkulloo was to induce the king to entrust him with the introduction of some cannon into the country. Whether he had succeeded or not I do not know, but he talked of returning again before long. We of course had no cabin accommodation, but were scattered about the deck wherever we could find room to stretch ourselves, and I consequently suffered considerably from the intense heat.

We progressed on the favourite Eastern principle of " still so gently," touching at every small island or projection of the mainland which came within our route, ostensibly with the object of taking in water and firewood, but more, I fancy, to please the captain, who had friends among the inhabitants of the occasional small fishing villages at which we stayed. I amused myself during the delays by bathing or strolling about the shores picking up shells and coral. These are amazingly abundant of every variety and great beauty. The shell of the cuttle-fish is strewn all over, as well as specimens of the beautiful white tree coral. Thousands of crabs and various-sized univalves make the beach appear as if alive. The coast is very barren, nothing but a few thorny trees and a species of kolquol, reduced to a mere shrub, are found to relieve the dreary waste. Brackish water is obtained by wells sunk into the sand.

The whole of this coast has a distinctively defined water-mark, about fifteen or twenty feet above the present high level of the sea, forming one in a chain of proofs, of which the extensive salt mines, abounding both on the Arabian and African shores of the Red Sea, and the salt lakes of Timsah in the Suez Isthmus are others, of the fact of this inland sea having had an extent in past ages much greater, and a level considerably higher, than at present; they would seem also to imply a former union with the Mediterranean and the consequent insulation of Africa.

Having for safety's sake skirted the mainland as far as we could consistently with our course, on the fourth day we struck out into the open sea, and getting an occasional run before a favourable wind, in four more days we sighted the Arabian coast, and soon after entered the " desired haven " of Hodeida. Several three-masted Calcutta merchantmen were lying off the town, bound for Jidda with rice, but detained here by contrary winds; and the sight of these fine vessels, contrasting so strongly with the miserable native craft by which they were surrounded, impressed my mind with a deep sense of the superiority of European civilisation, as well as of the progressive development of the Japhetic race compared with the stagnation of art and the supineness and inactivity of mind of our Shemitic and Hamitic brethren. But in approaching a country that was the cradle of a religion extending in the space of twelve centuries over a quarter of our globe, our sense of superiority in the arts and appliances of life is somewhat checked by the reflection, that the noble sentiment of religion has a deeper hold on the nature of these people than on ourselves; and it is a remarkable fact, that those religions which have started on the sublime recognition of the unity of the Godhead,—Judaism, Christianity, and Mohammedanism,—are Shemitic in their origin.

As Khawaja Yousef, the Syrian, had been in Hodeida before, and knew the place, I accompanied him into the town, to inspect it a little, and make inquiry as to the departure of a boat for Aden. Hodeida is a large, well-built town, containing a population of at least 50,000. The houses are built much after the Cairo model; and it possesses an excellent bazaar and market, with extensive Turkish cafés. It is walled and fortified, and has a large garrison of Turkish soldiers, who have an extremely sickly appearance, the effects of the excessive heat of the climate. Massowah is bad enough in this respect, but Hodeida is even much worse than Massowah. Most of the natives wear no clothing, except the waist-cloth; and yet, even while remaining perfectly inactive, the perspiration streams off the body. Nearly all the time is spent in lounging in the cafés, smoking the long *shibouk* or *argileh*, and drinking *kisheh*, a preparation of the leaf of the coffee plant. During the six days which intervened before another boat left for Aden, I was fain to spend the time at

Rome in the manner of the Romans, smoking, and drinking *kisheh*, like the rest. If

> " Satan find some mischief still
> For idle hands to do,"

he must have sufficient labour here, in Hodeida, if only in apportioning to others their work. But though I did nothing, it does not follow that I saw nothing; for when I could manage to keep my eyes open, I had abundant opportunities of witnessing many new phases of Oriental life here. The Arabs of Yemen, though possessing a bronze complexion, have very many of them reddish hair and beard, which gives them a somewhat curious appearance. They are tall and slenderly made, but their features differ from what we are apt to consider the pure Arab type; they are not so regular and so handsome. Their general dress consists of simply a blue-checked cloth thrown round the middle; but that of the respectable civilian, or shopkeeper, comprises of course a greater variety of articles, exceeding in gay appearance that of the similar class in Egypt, and showing a somewhat nearer approach to the costume of India. Indeed, India appears to be the market whence their wants are supplied, rather than from Europe, as is the case in Egypt.

In a general way it may be said, that the experience of ages has taught the natives of all countries the dress most adapted to the climate in which they live; and, unless there be political or other reasons against it, I think a European cannot do better than fall in with the customs of the people in this respect. It appeared extremely ludicrous to me to see here all the Turkish soldiers clothed in European costume,—tight trousers, close jacket, and heavy, thick-soled boots; the dress, even as an uniform, was the most inappropriate that could be imagined. The poor wretches seemed to writhe in agony, for the increased perspiration made the things stick closer than they otherwise would have done, and the consequence was, the breeches were always creeping up the legs, disclosing a pair of dirty stockings; and the sleeves up the arms, making the back of the jacket stick out horizontally. Really, the little respect which I had for the Turk in his fine native costume was almost ready to vanish at the sight of these caricatures. The Turks are very much hated by the Arabs of the interior, and it is with the utmost difficulty that they can maintain possession of a few seaports on the coast. The sultans of Sanaa, who rule this part of Yemen, have hitherto succeeded in efficaciously keeping them out of the interior; and I was told by a Turk here, that a party of them having once succeeded in reaching that capital were all massacred while worshipping in one of the mosques. Sanaa, about 200 miles from the coast, is said to be a beautiful city, containing some fine palaces, mosques, and fountains; but it is very difficult for a European to reach it, as the inhabitants are intensely bigoted Moslems.

I proposed to myself while here walking to Aden, for I encountered many difficulties in the endeavour to find a boat, but I was told that it would be unsafe, my informant accompanying his advice by the significant gesture of drawing his hand across his throat, to signify the probable result. A band of Turkish soldiers left just at this time for a town farther down on the coast, to compel by force of arms the payment of the required tribute.

Though the strip of land near the sea is hot and barren, the country in the interior, as it is set amongst high mountains (just discernible through the haze from the coast), is very rich and fruitful, answering fully to its title of Arabia Felix. I could easily credit what I was told of this from the variety of fruits which I saw in the market-place of Hodeida, including, amongst others, dates, bananas, figs, melons, lemons, pears, apples, peaches, and grapes. Grain also appears to be abundant, and is exported.

One source of amusement while seated in the cafés of Hoded a was the daily sale by auction of various articles, principally of clothing, which here takes place. A man with the article for sale in his hand walks the whole round of the bazaar, shouting out at the top of his voice, "*Ala bâb Allah, ala bâb el-kereem!*" "At the gate of God, at the gate of the Almighty!" This expression, which is only one of many, is, 1 suppose, intended to mean that he lays the article in question at the gate of God (Heaven), to be taken up by any one who will, as in the sight of the Almighty, give a fair price for it. It may also be intended to signify a dependence upon the good Providence of God in all the concerns of life. As he goes on he shouts out the last bid, adding on each extra amount as it is offered. This is a great break to the monotony of the smoke and coffee routine; and is the occasion of frequent sallies of wit on the part of the Arabs and Turks, both of whom are endowed with a keen sense of the ridiculous.

At noon the pangs of hunger induce an effort to

shunt off the *angareb* and shuffle away to some eating-house where, for about a piastre, your wants may be supplied. I daily went to the public kitchen of an old black, a native of Berber on the Nile, who had been in the service of Ibrahim Pasha in Syria and Asia Minor, and had at last reached this out-of-the-way place. He was an intelligent old fellow, and would sometimes bring my knowledge to bear in backing him out in an argument on geography with some obtuse native. He was delighted to hear that I had been in Bellad Soudan. The interval between dinner and supper is again occupied with coffee and pipe and a nap, and that between supper and bed-time by coffee and pipe again. I always slept in the front of some of the cafés; and, on getting up in the morning, sought at once the consolation of my coffee and pipe. One might have thought that, before a week was over, I should have got quite tired of this monotonous kind of life, but really it was quite otherwise; I could have kept at it for months. Indeed I don't see what else a person can do in such a climate; and I am sure I saw none who did anything else.

At length I succeeded in finding a boat to proceed; and, accompanied by Yousef and his wife, who had also taken a passage in the same vessel, went on board. Although informed that we should sail the same day, two or three days elapsed before we really left. We had a favourable north wind, and in a day and a half we reached Mocha. As our Nakhuda was a native of this place, he remained here a couple more days to see his family, and I had, therefore, an opportunity of looking over the town. I called a boat, and landed on the stone pier which runs out from the centre of the narrow bay on which Mocha is situated. A few Arab vessels were moored alongside. The aspect of the town from the sea is very dull; and this impression is not taken off when, on entering through the gate of the custom-house, you pass into the place itself. Full half the houses are uninhabited and in a very dilapidated condition, while the streets are almost empty, forming a marked contrast with the bustling appearance of Hodeida. I went into the bazaar to make a few purchases, and tasted on the spot the renowned Mocha coffee, for which I had to pay twice as much as elsewhere. Most Mocha coffee is, I believe, shipped at Hodeida: probably but a very small portion of the coffee which reaches us under that name is genuine. A gentleman once brought some samples of "real

Mocha" from a merchant at Liverpool who had himself received it as such, and on his arrival in these parts showed them to an extensive coffee merchant at Jidda, wishing his opinion as to their genuineness. This person, after a slight examination, at once pronounced them to be the production of Abyssinia; or, at least, not to be Mocha. As great quantities of Abyssinian coffee are exported from Massowah and Souakim, and in common with the Arabian coffee pass through Suez and Alexandria, the imposition is rendered quite easy; especially with persons who could not tell the difference when they saw the two together, as is doubtless the case with most dealers at home.

In addition to the bazaar there is also an open-air market outside the gates of the town: unfortunately, I was seduced into spending so much time here, that on my return I found the gates shut. The situation was rather awkward, as I was laden with a basket of provisions, with which I was about to return to the boat. I knew, however, that they would not sail before the morrow, so I was all right as far as that was concerned; but where should I stay the night? that was the question. I thought of my having slept in the cafés at Hodeida, and so resolved to try the same plan here.

I accordingly went and had a pot of *kisheh* at the nearest café I could find, and sat down to drink it to some bread and fruit which I had bought. This *kisheh*, as I have said, is a decoction of the coffee-leaf. The leaves are placed in a small earthen jar with a narrow neck, which is filled with water and is placed in the ashes of a charcoal fire. After having been allowed to boil some time, it is brought to you with a couple of small basins, or cups, into which you pour it as required. It has a peculiar taste, something between that of tea and coffee; but is very refreshing.

I now made bold to ask the proprietor of the café for permission to sleep there that night. He informed me that he did not live on the premises, but every night locked the place up and went home. He told me, however, that a quarter of a mile off there was another small door by which I might be able to re-enter the town. So, I trudged off in the direction pointed out, skirting the wall-side, and looking sharp out in the darkness to discover some traces of the door. Before long a man coming up asked who I was and what I was doing there; and on my reply he said the door was closed. It seemed certain that I should have to sleep where I was, and I proceeded to look out for a convenient spot for that purpose, when I saw at some short distance a man bearing a lantern. Making my way up to this fellow, I saw him, to my delight, pass through the very door I had been seeking. I ran up and asked the Turkish sentry to be admitted, explaining my circumstances and saying, that there was a Turkish café in the town where I thought I might sleep. He at once let me pass, and asked the man with the lantern to show me the way through the intricate streets to the café in question. Though it was not yet nine o'clock, all had retired to rest, and the streets were deserted, with the exception of some stray dog prowling about for refuse, who would bark at us furiously as we went by. At length we arrived near the café, and, recollecting the locality, I thanked my guide, assuring him he need not come any farther. I found an empty *angareb* in front of the café, and lay me down, hanging my basket of provisions near my head. I had not been here very long, however, before a man came up, demanding— "*Min hatha?*" "Who is this?" Though I was perfectly awake, I did not wish to be bothered with having to reply to the question, so I took no notice of him, feigning to be asleep. After repeating his question vainly, he at length walked off. I recomposed myself and was dozing nicely, when I both heard and felt something moving at my head. Slowly opening one eye, I perceived a large cat making a survey of the contents of my basket, to which it had been drawn by the smell of butcher's meat. Gently turning round, I let fly at it with my fist, but missed, for the animal was too sharp for me. I took the basket down, and endeavoured to find a convenient place for it, where these creatures (for several had now appeared) might not be able to get at it. I would have made a pillow of it, only it contained eggs amongst other things, and these I was afraid of squashing. I, therefore, managed by throwing my arms round it, and hugging it like a baby, to keep it out of the cats' clutches; though these thieves and beggars had sometimes the audacity to walk over me in order to get at it. When daybreak awoke me I found myself still cuddling my precious charge.

After coffee and a cigarette, which formed my breakfast, I went on board again, but we did not leave till the day after. Scudding before a favourable wind, in four hours we passed the straits of Bâb el-Mandeb (Gate of Tears), having the small island of Perim on our right. Though the place does not belong to us either by purchase or cession, we are suffered to occupy it, and it has an English garrison. It is perfectly barren, and has to be supplied with provisions from Aden. We were now in the Indian Ocean, and experienced a heavy swell, which is always the case here, probably occasioned by such a vast quantity of water at high tide having to pass through so narrow a strait. As the wind was high as well, though in our favour, our Nakhuda began to be rather timid, and ordered the sails to be reefed. The consequence was, that we were knocking about off the Arabian coast the whole of the succeeding night, whereas otherwise we might have reached Aden the same evening. The next morning the wind had abated a little, and so we made bold to set the sails again, and arrived off Aden at four in the afternoon; but, the wind blowing from the land, we were unable to enter the port. Consequently we were doomed to spend another night on the deep, but in the morning the wind had veered into the south-west, and in a couple of hours we reached the entrance of the western bay of Aden. How great was my delight when I saw the Union Jack flying over Steamer Point, and in the neat bungalows of the English residents, or some hotel or shop, saw the evident traces of civilisation, and those of my own beloved land!

R

APPENDIX.

THE ABYSSINIAN CAPTIVES QUESTION.

AFTER the complete and able statement of the Abyssinian question in Dr. Beke's recent work, it would be superfluous on my part to enter again into the details of the matter. I shall here content myself with a brief recapitulation of the unhappy events which have led to the present painful complication, adding thereto a few remarks of my own on the differences between King Theodore and our Government, on the chances of a settlement, and on the probable bearing of such a settlement upon the future of Abyssinia.

I. RÉSUMÉ OF MAIN INCIDENTS.—I have before shown how Theodore by the force of his genius (and notwithstanding recent events it would be vain to deny him the possession of remarkable genius), had succeeded in raising himself from the position of a private soldier to the highest dignity in the state, and in re-uniting under his sway the scattered provinces of the empire. I have also shown how, antecedent to the undertaking of his scheme of conquest, whose immediate object was the rescue of the outly ng provinces, now in the power of Egypt (the sea-board, Bogos, Gellabat, &c., over which territory he had a perfectly just right), he first sought to obtain the recognition, by the nations of Europe, of his title to the throne of Abyssinia. From the letter given on pp. 155-6, it will be seen that he did not require more than this, and that though he there attempts to justify his purpose of making war on the Turks, such was not the main object of his letter, but that he simply sought to ascertain the willingness of England, as in a similar letter he wished to know that of France, to receive and guarantee the safe passage through Egypt of the ambassadors which he proposed to send. It was an unimpeachable letter, and it required and deserved a fitting answer. That Theodore did not doubt of its favourable reception is evidenced by the fact of his immediately giving orders for the preparation of those presents which he intended should accompany his em-bassy. That such was also the view in which Captain

Cameron, our representative, regarded the matter, is proved by his return, after seeing its safe despatch, to the king's court, there to await the answer and to hold himself in readiness (his health not allowing him to retain his post) to accompany Theodore's embassy to England. In order to make provision against any possible delay in its transmission to him on arrival at Massowah, he left at that port Mr. Kerens, his secretary, and Mertcha, dragoman to the consulate, with orders to bring it up immediately they received it; and, as has been seen, when I left Massowah these two were, as it were, momentarily listening for the salute of the " Victoria " gunboat, which was to bring it from Aden. Poor Kerens! He anticipated with great pleasure his visit to the court of King Theodore, and showed me some fire-arms and a handsome carpet, representing Jules Gérard, the African lion-hunter, which he intended as presents to the monarch. Could he have anticipated the reception he and his presents would receive, he would have looked forward to his interview with very different feelings!

Four months after my departure, and a full twelve-month from the despatch of the king's letter, the longed-for despatches arrived, and with ready haste .Kerens

and Mertcha proceeded to rejoin Captain Cameron at
Gondar. Our consul, who, on account of a journey
through the Egyptian provinces on the north, had
rather forfeited his favour with the king, thought that
now all would be made right. It was, no doubt, with
joyful anticipation that Captain Cameron opened the
long-expected despatches; but what was his amazement
when, instead of a letter expressing the Queen's willingness to receive Theodore's embassy, he only received
one addressed to himself, containing an unjust reproof
for meddling in Abyssinian affairs, and a peremptory
order to go to his post at Massowah.

The king's letter had absolutely not been deemed
worthy of notice by the English minister. The consul's
position was thus rendered extremely painful. By acting
up to the instructions of our own Government in making
the journey to Kassala and Gellabat, he had displeased
the king; and by his journey to Bogos, in accordance
with the wish of the king, he had displeased his own
Government; and now he had to face the monarch with
the intelligence of his letter being ignored, which of
course was equivalent to our having refused to entertain
his embassy. The result was as might have been expected from an offended barbarian prince. The king

took the reprisals which, in his position, lay open to him, he seized the persons of all the British subjects in his dominions, the consul included, with the intimation as shown in Captain Cameron's first letter home, that there would be "no release until a civil answer to the king's letter arrived."*

If the Christian maxim "Confess your faults one to another," had been deemed as binding on princes and states as it is on private individuals, a great deal of the bloodshed which has deluged the world might have been spared : at least this perilous and costly war upon which we are now about to enter, might possibly have been averted : but it is a tradition with our Foreign Office to maintain an alliance with the Turks, and Theodore is the enemy of the Turks, so Mr. Layard, who has a great friendship for the Turks, must be accused of having for once cast aside his sagacity and prudence; and it has, we know, always been difficult for Earl Russell to retrace a step, or even indicate an

* It will be seen that I have not entered at all into Stern's affair, for I am here principally tracing the origin of the king's quarrel with our Government, with which Stern's original ill-treatment had nothing to do. I believe he would have been liberated long since had he not afterwards, as a British subject, been doomed to share the fate of the rest.

apology that confesses to a false move.   The fact was, that Theodore's character, his power and his aims, were not comprehended either by Earl Russell or Mr. Layard —to suppose not, is but just to the latter gentleman.

Had her Majesty subsequently been advised to soften the mind of the African by the obvious, though perhaps irregular expedient, of answering Theodore's letter with her own royal hand, the blunder might have been redeemed by an expression of the Queen's willingness to receive both embassy and presents, and the deputing of Consul Cameron to conduct the same to England. Our Government decided that her Majesty ought not to be advised to write to the King of Abyssinia.   In that decision they assumed a terrible responsibility. When public opinion and the voice of Parliament had for some time persisted in urging a contrary course, Earl Russell consented to re-open a correspondence with Theodore.   But even after this resolution had been framed, the letter which her Majesty was requested to write was not a reply to the king's, for the main subject of Theodore's epistle—*the question of our receiving his ambassadors*—does not appear to have been so much as mentioned.   Presuming that Earl Russell meant to act seriously, he was guilty of a great mistake, for had we declared that we were ready to receive the ambassadors of the King of Abyssinia, Theodore would probably have sent them forthwith, even if he had retained (as he has done) our own; and we should by that means at least have had some guarantee for the safety of our countrymen; whereas now we have none.

However, as it had been resolved to write to Theodore, the next consideration was, Who should be the bearer of these despatches? There were many applications for the delicate, and, as it has turned out to be since, dangerous post, amongst others one by the writer of these pages, who having just returned from the country, and having been well received by the king, was prepared to take the risk, whatever it might be, which appeared to attach to the mission. Perhaps the most likely person of all was Major Plowden, cousin to the late consul, the king's friend, for the high respect Theodore ever bore to the latter, would have almost certainly ensured a favourable reception to an officer bearing the same name and claiming close relationship with the deceased friend of the king. Dr. Beke also had a very great claim upon the attention of the Government; his knowledge of the country, its languages, manners and customs, peculiarly fitted him for the task. All,

however, had to give way to Mr. Rassam, the assistant
to the Political Resident of Aden, a gentleman who,
though the wisdom of his appointment was much called
in question at the time, has since, in his transactions
with Theodore, showed an amount of prudence and tact
which, in my opinion, no other could have surpassed, if
equalled, him in. Owing, however, to delays of one
kind or another, inexcusable both in Mr. Rassam and
others concerned, it was not till January, 1866, more
than two years after our countrymen's first imprisonment, that he arrived in the king's cam .

The report Mr. Rassam has given of his reception by
Theodore is rather a strange document, and appears to
have been written under a probability of its being intercepted and read by the king. He was received with all
the state due to an envoy of her Majesty, greeted with
almost regal honours, and overwhelmed with presents,
including amongst the rest a sum of 15,000 dollars, to
be spent in any manner he wished, "except in a way
displeasing to God." His daily wants and necessities,
with those of his retinue, were supplied in a most sump-
tuous manner, sometimes reaching as much as one
thousand loaves of bread, two cows, twenty fowls, five
hundred eggs, ten jars of milk, ten of honey, &c. In-

deed, such was the apparent friendliness of his reception at the hands of the king, that he himself says: "Everyone, therefore, whether European or Abyssinian, admitted that no sovereign could be more attentive and gracious to the representative of a foreign government than Theodore of Abyssinia was to Mr. Rassam."

With regard to the object of his mission, Mr. Rassam relates that, "after the king had thrown all the blame on the missionaries and Captain Cameron for having by their conduct caused the breach between him and the British Government [?], he was pleased to release the captives in consideration of the new friendship Mr. Rassam had succeeded in establishing between him and our Queen."

In accordance with this decision an order was sent forward to Magdala for the chains of the prisoners to be knocked off, and for the whole of them to be brought to Gorata, on Lake Tsana, where Mr. Rassam was to take up his quarters till their arrival. When this took place Mr. Rassam says that the king wished to see the released prisoners for the purpose of getting them to acknowledge the justice of the punishment which they had received, but that, fearing something might arise to irritate the emperor, Mr. Rassam begged him to dispense with their presence. This the king agreed to, and he stated that he was prepared to allow the matter to be tried before Mr. Rassam, the European workmen of Gaffat, and a number of his own officers. In this court the captives, says Mr. Rassam, confessed that they had done wrong, and begged his Majesty to forgive them, whereupon Theodore restored to them his favour.

Mr. Rassam's report concludes by saying " that the emperor then ordered the translation of her Majesty's letter, and his answer thereto, to be read publicly by the chief scribe. Then all heard what had been written in his letter." Mr. Rassam proceeds to quote some passages from the same, but as I think the document is very interesting as proving the king's intentions at the time, it may be as well to give it here in full:

"In the name of the Father, of the Son, and of the Holy Ghost, one God. Amen.

"From the servant of Our Lord, and His created being, the son of David, the son of Solomon, the Kin of Kings (of Ethiopia), Theodorus,

"To her, whom God has exalted above all sovereigns and glorified above all princes and peoples, and made the Defender of the Christian Faith, and the succour of the poor and oppressed, Victoria, Queen of the United Kingdom of Great Britain and Ireland:

"Had the illustrious Hormuzd Rassam, whom your Majesty has mentioned to us in your letter, not been sent to us about the matter of Cameron and others, but the lowest of your servants, he would have been received graciously by us. *We now send with Hormuzd Rassam, Cameron and all the other Europeans about whom your Majesty has written.* Your Majesty can learn from those who fear the Lord the ill-treatment and abuse which we have received at the hands of the above-mentioned Europeans, and the Copt, who called himself Metropolitan, the Aboona Salama.

" In my humble position I am not worthy to address your Majesty, but illustrious princes and the deep ocean can bear everything. I, being an ignorant Ethiopian, hope that your Majesty will overlook my shortcomings and pardon my faults. The people whom we have imprisoned for their reviling and defaming us did so because the Gallas had proved victorious over the royal children of Israel and had humbled them; but God has empowered me, the son of one of the humble women of Israel, to regain that which had been lost by my forefathers.

"Doubtless your Majesty has learnt how ignorant and blind the people of Ethiopia are; wherefore I beg of your Majesty not to take amiss the mistakes I may make in my correspondence with you. Counsel me, but do not blame me, O Queen, whose majesty God has glorified, and to whom he has given abundance of wisdom.

"Dated the 22nd day of January, 1858" (corresponding to the 29th of January, 1866).*

Dr. Beke, arguing from what took place so soon afterwards, is inclined to look upon this letter as a mere mockery, and not as a sincere expression of the king's heart, but for my own part I must say I think he meant what he said at the time of his saying it. Indeed I can imagine no conceivable object in the kind treatment given by the king to our envoy, if it was not that he was really desirous of re-establishing a good feeling between the government of Great Britain and himself. In addition to this letter, his good intentions appear also to be testified by the fact of his giving orders both to his European workmen at Gaffat, and his Armenian silversmiths, for the preparation of some rich presents

* Abyssinian Blue Book, 1867.

intended for our Queen. Surely this was not all mockery too?

I am inclined, therefore, to think that all would have ended satisfactorily had it not been for the devilish machinations of some persons in the king's court, who afterwards infused into his mind the suspicion that, when our countrymen had safely reached the frontier, the British Government would then be revenged on him for their previous ill-treatment. The persons who were at the root of all this mischief were two principally, Aito Samuel, "the emperor's steward," a native of the country, then much in favour with his Majesty, and of whom I shall have to speak afterwards; and M. Bardel, a Frenchman, who had entered Abyssinia in the service of Captain Cameron, but had afterwards quarrelled with him. M. Bardel, as I have previously remarked (p. 155), was the bearer of the king's letter to Napoleon, and also had brought back Napoleon's reply; since which time he has used all manner of intrigues to prejudice the king's mind against English and Protestants, and in favour of the French and Jesuits. He has been in regular correspondence all along with Padre Delmonte, an intriguing Jesuit at Massowah, who has been known to furnish him with English documents, Government despatches, and newspapers, which Bardel has translated to the king. It is surely to be hoped that this vile wretch, who has thus played with the lives of our countrymen, may eventually be brought to some kind of justice, or at least that his conduct may be held up to public execration.

The result of the plotting of these two intriguers was that the king was determined to retain a guarantee for our future good conduct towards him; and with this idea he hit upon a scheme which he thought would answer his purpose. On the strength of a passage in the Queen's letter (a mistranslation, it has been said), whereby her Majesty was represented as saying that everything the king wished Mr. Rassam would do for him, he expressed his desire to have a number of English artisans who would instruct his people in the manufacture of cannon, muskets, &c. He therefore proposed that the released prisoners should be sent on their way, and on their arrival in England arrangements should be made for the despatch of these artizans to Abyssinia, Mr. Rassam remaining in the meanwhile as a hostage, or, as the king put it, to " consult further on the extension of their friendship." Mr. Rassam natu-rally objected to the proposition, on the ground that such a course would not be consistent with the instructions he had received from our Government. The refusal no doubt tended to increase the king's suspicion, but he concealed his thoughts, and still treated Mr. Rassam well, until the day came when the prisoners were to have departed. It was the 13th of April. On that day it was arranged that Mr. Rassam and party should cross over from Gorata, on the eastern side of Lake Tsana, where they had been residing, to Zagyé, on the western shore, where the king held his camp, to take leave of his Majesty before their departure. In the meanwhile the released prisoners were to proceed on their way to the frontier, to be afterwards rejoined on the road by Mr. Rassam. The arrangement appears to have been agreed to by Theodore himself, though he afterwards made out that he wished Mr. Rassam to bring them to him to be personally reconciled before leaving. However this may have been, it is evident that he had come to the determination not to let them depart just then. No sooner had Mr. Rassam and the other members of the mission arrived at the king's camp than they were immediately arrested, and the poor captives, on reaching a village some two hours' journey from Gorata, shared the same fate, being there seized by Dejage Tadla, a governor of Theodore's, who had received an order from the king to the following effect: "We have been angry with our friends and with those Europeans who say, ' We go to our country, and are not yet reconciled.' Until we consult what we are going to do, take hold of them, but do not make them uncomfortable and afraid, and do not hurt them."

From the expression here used, it would appear that the king then had really not made up his mind what he would do, and it has been said that a day or two after, when he had once more been reconciled to them, he further pledged his word that he would instantly grant the captives their freedom if Mr. Rassam would consent to stay behind. This gentleman, however, although Dr. Blanc offered to stay with him, still would not submit to this arrangement, and the consequence was they were all detained. It is just to remark that they were treated with every kindness and attention.

About this time an incident took place which gives a strange picture of King Theodore's character. If Dr. Beke would only give the king credit for a little more sincerity, it might form a conclusive refutation of many unjust charges that have lately been made against himself, proving the good effect his mission, had it been fully carried out, would probably have produced. I give it in the words of Mr. Flad:

"In the morning on the 17th [April] we were called to the tent of Mr. Rassam. Soon after we arrived there the king sent a message to Mr. Rassam that our chains should be opened. After about an hour, which we spent in the tent of Mr. Rassam, the three English gentlemen received from his Majesty an invitation to an audience. We (the released prisoners) were also ordered to appear. As soon as we (the prisoners) had approached near his Majesty and received his salutation, we fell down to the ground, asking his Majesty to forgive and to pardon us. We were ordered to get up and to come nearer. We had the honour to take a seat on a carpet. The king brought forth the petition of the relations of the English prisoners, which had been sent from Massowah by Dr. Beke. Captain Cameron was asked to read it. After that the king said: 'It is the devil who made me angry with you, and who tempted me to destroy the friendly feelings existing since the late Mr. Plowden between myself and England. From my childhood I like the Europeans, especially the English, and God knows that from morning till evening I had no other desire than to get in alliance with the English nation. It is true that by the power of God I will fight the Turks, but there never arose a thought in my mind to fight the English. What I wish is that they shall love me and be my friends. Mr. Stern,' said he, 'you are quite innocent ; it is not you who abused me—it is that Copt, who calls himself a monk and a bishop. He made me angry with you, and he abused me. And Mr. Flad, God knows I never had any bad feelings against him. He never committed anything which could make me angry with him. And Mr. Rassam, you are the best man I ever saw in my life, and you did nothing which could make me angry with you. The other day, it is true, my suspicion arose, but it was the devil, and now we will make peace, forgetting everything past, and by actions of love we will renew our friendship.' The king immediately fell down to the ground before us. We asked that his Majesty might arise and forgive us, but he refused. So we said, according to the custom of the country, 'For God's sake, we forgive you,' and immediately we kneeled down before him, begging him to forgive us; on which he answered, 'For God's sake, I forgive you.' After this ceremony we had to sit down. Then the king said that each of us should write a letter to his relations, and give them news that his Majesty, by the power of God, and for the friendship sake of the Queen of England, had pardoned and released us, and that we hoped to see and meet them soon. After this we were dismissed."

To those who are accustomed to see in Theodore nothing but the " bloodthirsty tyrant " of whom we have heard so much of late, the above strange scene will appear almost incredible, or at all events get for him the credit of hypocrisy in addition to the other ugly features of his character ; but others, who have taken a more favourable if not a juster view of Theodore, would find in this incident a proof that he is possessed of a few good qualities that occasionally crop out, and, though they are only the flash of a moment, form a relief to the general darkness. Nor are these sudden transitions of feeling peculiar to Theodore : they are in a great measure common to all Orientals, and such inconsistencies in the character of these people are often a matter of perplexity to European travellers, who, rather than attempt the difficult task of reconciling them, cut the gordian knot by taking a one-sided view of the subject, and wilfully blinding their eyes to the other. Hence, according to the aspect first presented to their view, or according to the temper and quality of the minds of the travellers themselves, we have the most irreconcileable descriptions of the same people, or even of the very same individuals. The modern Egyptians, for instance, have been studied by innumerable travellers, and while the generality of them agree in painting them, if not in the blackest hue, at all events in "sepia," others, like Lady Duff Gordon, use only the pigment called *couleur de rose*. So with individuals; and we have a most remarkable case in point in the famous "Samuel, the emperor's (Theodore's) steward." Bishop Gobat, in his "Journal of Missionary Work in Abyssinia" in 1833, speaks of him as the most sincere and likely convert he had made, and no doubt rejoiced that in this instance he had some reward for his labour. Dr. Krapf, who knew him a few years later, says he was an intriguer from his youth; and Dr. Beke, whose servant he was, had pretty much the same opinion. Mr. Waldmaier told me he was the greatest rascal in the country, and Mr. Flad warned Mr. Rassam on entering the country not to trust him, as being a most dangerous character. Mr. Stern, who had more experience of him than any other, calls him a "compound of hatred, malice, and cunning," "a hypocrite," "a messenger of evil," " a smooth, flattering knave," &c. ; and yet, as if obliged to give another testimony, he relates incidents which seem to show that he was occasionally ruled by a higher class of feelings. He mentions how in one instance he " crouched down near Captain Cameron and with the utmost assiduity tended his wounds." On another occasion, speaking of his own sufferings, caused in a great measure by Samuel himself, he says, " As I could not move, Samuel, *with great tenderness*, held the cup to my fevered lips."

Again, notwithstanding that it was well known that he had been the root of nearly all the evil which has happened to our countrymen during their long imprisonment, acting as the king's spy at the same time that he received bribes from the prisoners to act in their interests, Mr. Rassam in the face of this knowledge tells us that Samuel " seemed really desirous of promoting a friendly feeling between England and Abyssinia." To add to all, and make the paradox perfect, the prisoners themselves, in the latest letters received from them, actually speak of the many good services he has rendered them during their imprisonment, adducing such as a guarantee of his sincerity. Mr. Rassam says, " Samuel has lost the greater part of the royal favour, because it has been proved that he favoured the English. The fact is, there is no man in the country who is so faithful to his liege as this Samuel; and because he has been trying all he could to benefit his royal master by getting him to be on good terms with us, he is distrusted. Some of the released prisoners used to think that he was implicated in their former trials. However that may have been, his honest, friendly feeling towards the British has been proved to me beyond doubt. That he is anything but unfriendly towards us, though he considers himself bound to love and obey his sovereign, I have lately been able to prove to both Cameron and Stern."

" These two gentlemen," adds Colonel Merewether, " have written to me that they are quite convinced of Samuel's probity now, and Dr. Blanc says the same." *

I might adduce other instances of similar characters I have known, all of which would go to prove that amongst Orientals one finds the most strange compounds. But none which might be adduced would compare with King Theodore himself, in whom the principles of good and evil are so mysteriously mixed that

* " Further Correspondence relating to British Captives in Abyssinia, 1867," p. 132.

he might be a devil and an angel in one person. The barbarous cruelties and reckless bloodsheddings which have lately characterised his reign, would certainly entitle him to a place among the Herods, the Neros, or the Borgias, and give him a just title to be mentioned in the same breath with a King of Dahomey; but, on the other hand, the kindness, the generosity, the tenderness, the gentleness, which at various times he has displayed, would by themselves claim a niche for him among the good kings of the earth. But not only in the various passions of our nature has he shown this fearful contrast: the powers of his mind evince the same inconsistencies; wisdom and childishness, prudence and recklessness, religion and profanity, are intermingled in the chaos of his intellect. Even pride, which is his ruling passion, as it is that of Abyssinians in general, sometimes yields to the most profound humility, as in a certain manner shown in the words of the letter to our Queen before quoted.

It is related (though it would seem almost incredible) that once in the fullness of his pride he said, " I have made a bargain with God; He has promised not to descend on earth to strike me, and I have promised not to ascend into heaven to fight with Him." In contrast to this he has often said, " Without Christ I am nothing ; by the power of God, who raised me up from the dust, I have done what I have done."

We have these indications to prove that the impulses of good and evil which exist in him do not in any way blend with or influence each other. The qualities of the mind or functions of the brain seem to act independently. When one passion is exerting itself, all the rest are dormant. If he is under the influence of certain feelings, be they good or bad, no other consideration is advanced to interfere with their exercise. Hence, for the time being, he is a kind of monomaniac, acting at one moment like a tiger, the next like a lamb; a devil to-day, and a saint to-morrow.

From these inconsistencies in King Theodore's character, it is not surprising that some persons should look upon him as a madman. Earl Russell, in a communication once made by his lordship to Dr. Beke, said that he had been led to the conclusion that " Theodore could not be in his right mind." Perhaps not ; but, in my opinion, his is a kind of mania which is very common in the East, the only difference between Theodore and other Orientals being that in him it assumed a more virulent form. His mind was more powerful than theirs; consequently, the peculiarities which marked them were in him more marked. But if he was "touched" either by the fire of genius or by that of madness (it is often hard to distinguish between the two), so much greater the necessity for a "keeper;" in other words, for good and wise counsellors, who could check his wildness, and direct his powerful energies into their proper channel. Theodore had one formerly; a faithful guardian, though his servant—bosom-companion to a king, though a subject. But him he lost, and in losing him lost his throne, his kingdom, himself. He feels it, and he has acknowledged it repeatedly. No one came forward to take that "keeper's" place, because no one was prepared to offer a life's devotion to his "charge;" and so the madman was left to himself, and destroyed himself, but, Samson-like, would not die alone.

The king now reverted to an original project which he had of sending Mr. Flad to England, with the object of obtaining for him the artisans and machinery he has been for the last ten years longing to possess. He thought, also, that in the persons of the English artisans he would have the hostages he required against any reprisals on our part for his previous treatment of British subjects. But he did not wish it to appear as if this idea had originated in himself, but more as if it proceeded from Mr. Rassam. Hence he got Mr. Rassam to write to our Government to have these persons forwarded, almost dictating to him his letter. He also wrote himself to our Queen, stating that he had released all the prisoners, and made them over to Mr. Rassam, and that he kept the latter "for the sake of consulting together upon the extension of our friendship."

Mr. Flad left the king's court on the 21st of April, 1866, proceeding thence by way of Matammah and Kassala to Massowah, where he arrived on the 31st of May. Thence he proceeded to Aden, and so on to Suez, Alexandria, and England, arriving here in July.

The Government of Lord Derby, in a spirit of moderation which Theodore had certainly no right to expect, proceeded at once to assist Mr. Flad in obtaining the artisans and machinery the king wished, and he was also furnished with another letter from the Queen to the Emperor Theodore; her Majesty further granting him the honour of an audience, as it was thought that the king would be pleased to hear that Mr. Flad had been thus honoured. But although the Government still adopted a conciliatory course, it was thought desirable that the artisans should not be allowed to enter

Abyssinia before the Europeans there detained had been first sent to the frontier; and her Majesty was accordingly asked to make this stipulation in her letter to the emperor.

Owing to the necessary delay attending the preparation of the machinery intended for the king, Mr. Flad did not succeed in leaving till the 9th of October, being then accompanied by the artisans who had been engaged for the king's service. In the meanwhile, however, the sad news reached England that, some two months after Flad's departure, the whole of the prisoners, Rassam and his party included, had been again consigned to chains in the fortress of Magdala. Up to that time (June) they had been treated with the greatest kindness, and the reason for this strange turn in their fortunes was that the king had heard that England was having constructed a railroad from Souakim to Kassala, with the object of conveying by that means a joint army of English and Egyptians for the purpose of attacking his territory. He had also heard from Abyssinians at Jerusalem that Mr. Rassam had been sent out on false pretences, and that England had no good intentions towards him; and, furthermore, an European (no doubt Padre Delmonte, the Jesuit) had written to him from

Massowah, telling him that "the English Government wanted nothing but his utter ruin."

The sudden return of Dr. Beke from Massowah was also thought to have something to do with it, though in what way is difficult to say, unless Theodore was led to believe that he had been recalled by our own Government. There was sufficient, however, in these reports to enable Bardel, the Frenchman, and Samuel, "the emperor's steward," to work sufficiently on the mind of the king to obtain the result they wished, the disgrace and renewed imprisonment of our countrymen.

In the meanwhile Mr. Flad, continuing his journey, arrived on the 29th of October at Massowah, whence he despatched, by four different messengers, copies in Amharic and English of her Majesty's letter to Theodore, as well as a letter of his own explaining why the artisans could not be sent forward before the prisoners were released. These letters reached the king about the 19th of December, and on receipt of them he wrote to Mr. Rassam, sending a copy of her Majesty's letter, and saying he was about to visit him to consult with him as to the answer he should send. For some reasons, however, he was unable to do this, and a few days after he wrote again to Mr. Rassam, saying that the following was the answer he proposed to return:

" Formerly England and Ethiopia were on terms of friendship, and I also, having knowledge of this, used to love you exceedingly. But, since then, having heard that they (the English) have calumniated and hated me with the Turks, I said to myself, ' Can this be true?' and I felt some misgiving in my heart. However, I trust there is no enmity between Ethiopia and the English, but that there is friendship. We do not esteem those who calumniate and hate the English, and so should you, for our sake, not esteem those who calumniate and hate the people of Ethiopia. Mr. Rassam and his party, whom you sent to me, I have placed in my house, in my capital at Magdala, and I will treat them well, until I obtain a token of your friendship."*

Immediately after this he wrote further to Mr. Rassam, the following being extracts from his letter:

" Now, in order to prove the good relationship between me and yourself, let it be shown by your writing, and getting the skilful artisans and Mr. Flad to come by

---

* It must be remembered that chains are not looked at in the light of a punishment in Abyssinia, but as a means to prevent escape.

way of Matammah. This will be the sign of our friendship. When you hate my enemies and love my friends, and I shall prove wanting in my friendship towards you, leave me to God (as my Judge). . . . . I wish you to get them (the skilful artisans) by way of Matammah, in order that they may teach me wisdom and show me clever arts. When this is done, I shall make you glad, and send you away by the power of God."

From this it will be seen what use the king intends making of Mr. Rassam, and certainly his is not a very enviable position. However, hitherto he has displayed the greatest coolness and judgment, and it is to be hoped that this may still carry both him and the captives through the fiery ordeal which seems before them.

Although the above is the reply Theodore proposed to make to the letter of her Majesty of October 4, 1866, of which Mr. Flad sent the copies, it is not publicly known whether King Theodore really forwarded his reply to the proper authorities ; but, whether the original has been received by our Government or not, the king's refusal to comply with the wishes of our Queen, by releasing the prisoners, was deemed sufficient to convince the Government that further negotiations were useless, and Lord Stanley, accordingly, on the 16th of April last, sent an ultimatum, or a letter which is equivalent to one, to the troublesome monarch, in which, three months from the date of its despatch from Massowah were allowed to the king to have our countrymen conveyed to his frontiers. This term expired on the 17th of August last. The Government are therefore now at liberty to take forcible measures for the liberation of the Europeans so unjustly detained by King Theodore.

Continuing, however, the narrative of all the unhappy events connected with this vexed question, it is necessary to say that Mr. Flad was detained at Massowah, waiting for permission to enter, till the 6th of March of the present year, at which date he left that place for Matammah, where he arrived on the 29th. Here, however, he was further detained, owing to the road between that place and Debra Tabor being occupied by rebels of Tessu Góbasie's party. From this spot, however, he wrote to his Majesty; and whatever may have been the subject of his letter, there was something in it which put the king into such bad humour that on some frivolous pretence he had the whole of his European workmen at Gaffat seized and brought as prisoners to Debra Tabor. What was the cause of this harsh treatment of those

T

whom he had hitherto considered his best friends, and who had served him throughout so faithfully, it is hard to say. None of them dared write to explain the matter; but Mr. Waldmaier, in a verbal message to Mr. Rassam, says that it was owing to their having been aware of some military preparations which were being made on his frontiers, and having nevertheless concealed their knowledge of this from him. The following is the account given by Dr. Blanc of the affair, gathered from native report:

"On the 17th [April] his Majesty proceeded to Gaffat, called the Europeans before him (with the exceptions of Messrs. Schimper and Zander), ordered all their property to be seized, and removed them prisoners to Debra Tabor. When he came to Gaffat, his Majesty remained in the factory below the hill on which Gaffat is built. On the arrival of the Europeans, he told them that he had received a letter from Flad, containing many things, and that, until confirmed by Flad, he could not trust them, and must therefore keep them near him. He said that he had also heard that preparations for the reception of troops had been made at   , and that if he was to be killed, they would die first; but, added he, 'Do not be afraid' (the usual expression when he means mischief), 'you are my children,' &c. Some of the Europeans, especially Mr. Maurice Hall [Herr Moritz, the Pole], remonstrated strongly with his Majesty, asking him why, after serving him so many years faithfully, they were subjected to such an unjust treatment. ' Kill us at once,' said Hall, 'but do not degrade us in this way; if in the letter you have received there is anything you can charge against us, then cause it to be read out before all your people; death is better than unjust suspicion.' His Majesty, in an angry tone, ordered him to be quiet, sent them to Debra Tabor under escort, and had tents pitched for them in the plain, at the foot of the hill on which the royal residence is built." Dr. Blanc further adds, "Gaffat is now entirely deserted, the workshops demolished, and not a servant allowed to remain to take care of the houses."

It was not until the king had moved his troops in the direction of Matammah, that the rebel party of Tessu Góbasie retreated, and left the road open for Mr. Flad to pursue his journey to the king's capital. His arrival and reception by the king is thus related in a letter of Mr. Rosenthal's, which appeared in the *Times* of the 9th of August:

" Mr. Flad arrived at Debra Tabor on the 4th of May. After being introduced to the king, his Majesty asked him, ' Where are the workmen ? ' To which Mr. Flad replied, ' I would have brought them straight up, if your Majesty had not imprisoned Mr. Rassam and his companions.' ' For the matter of that,' sulkily answered the king, ' the artisans would not have come, even if I had not chained them.' Among the presents which were offered there was a telescope, which did not at all meet with the approbation of the monarch, although it is said to be excellent of its kind. ' I desired to have my eyes opened,' said his Majesty, ' and is this the way of doing it, by sending me a bad telescope ? I cannot see anything at all through it. Some years ago Lieutenant Speedy conveyed to me a small carpet through Mr. Kerens, and, by the power of God, I chained the bearer. This telescope has also been brought to me for evil, and I shall do the same to the donor.'

" His Majesty then inquired about the future intentions of England in reference to himself; upon which Mr. Flad informed him that he could not expect any more friendship if he did not allow the European prisoners at once to depart. ' Let them come,' replied the king, ' and call me a woman if I do not fight them ' (a boast which no one now believes), adding, ' Those who have faith like a grain of mustard-seed shall be able to remove mountains.'

" When the audience was over, Mr. Flad was ordered to repair to his tent, but he did not receive any rations from the royal kitchen for the two following days, a clear intimation to all that Mr. Flad was not in favour. On the Abyssinian Easter-day, however, a cow was sent to Mr. Flad, with the command to come to the king. The same ludicrous scene with the telescope was performed over again, without success. The glass would not suit his Majesty's eyes at all. On this occasion Mr. Flad informed the king that he had something more to tell him; and when permitted to speak said, ' England was always friendly towards you, and is so even now. Lately Waagshum Góbasie, the Tigrean rebel, sent to say that he would liberate the Europeans from Magdala on condition that the English would befriend him in future. This proposal was not accepted, but answered that the English could recognise but one king in a country, and held no communication with rebels.' ' I know,' replied the king, ' that the English were never amicably disposed towards me, not even at the time of Bell and Consul Plowden; but the latter were my personal friends.' On dismissal, Mr. Flad was told to join his family."

It will thus be seen that the whole of the Europeans in Theodore's territory, with the exception of Messrs. Bardel, Zander, and Schimper, are now prisoners at the mercy of the king.* Mr. Flad, when in England, gave their numbers as sixty-one, including their wives and families. There are, consequently, now sixty-two; this brave and noble-hearted man having, rather than forsake his wife and children, thus heroically joined their number. The following is a list, which I believe is correct :

AT MAGDALA.

Mr. Rassam, Her Britannic Majesty's Envoy, Ottoman.†

Dr. Blanc, Physician, English.

Lieutenant Prideaux, Assistant, English.

Captain Cameron, Her Britannic Majesty's Consul for Abyssinia, English.

Mr. Kerens, Secretary to Captain Cameron, English.

Mr. M'Kilvie, servant to Captain Cameron, English.

---

* Later reports state that the Gaffat artisans are again in favour.
† So given in Parliamentary Papers.

Pietro, servant to Captain Cameron, Italian.

Rev. H. A. Stern, Missionary from London Society for Promoting Christianity amongst the Jews, German.

Mr. Rosenthal, Lay Missionary from London Society for Promoting Christianity amongst the Jews, German.

At Debra Tabor.

Rev. M. Flad, wife and children, Missionary from the London Society for Promoting Christianity amongst the Jews, German.

Rev. — Bender, wife and children, Missionary from the Pilgrims' Mission, Basle, German.

Mr. Waldmaier, wife and children, Lay Missionary from the Pilgrims' Mission, Basle, German.

Mr. Saalsmüller, wife and children, Lay Missionary from the Pilgrims' Mission, Basle, German.

Mr. Mayer, wife and children, Lay Missionary from the Pilgrims' Mission, Basle, German.

Mr. Steiger, Lay Missionary from the Scotch Society for Promoting Christianity amongst the Jews, German.

Mr. Brandeis, Lay Missionary from the Scotch Society for Promoting Christianity amongst the Jews, German.

Mr. Schiller, Adventurer, German.

Mr. Essler, Adventurer, German.

Herr Moritz (Maurice Hall), Adventurer, Polish.

M. Makerer, Adventurer, French.

M. Bourgaud, Gunsmith, French.

Mrs. Kiensle and child, wife of deceased Missionary of Pilgrims' Mission, Basle, German.

Mrs. Rosenthal and child, wife of Mr. Rosenthal, English.

II. How to settle the "Question."—The question now comes upon us with overwhelming force: What must be done for the liberation of all these Europeans whom the quarrel between Theodore and our Government has caused to be deprived of their liberty?

The answer which every Englishman would give, and the answer which the Government, anticipating the voice of the nation, has already given, is, We must compel their liberation by the force of our arms. However wrong the Government of Earl Russell may have been originally in refusing a reply to the civil letter of King Theodore, the conciliatory course which has been adopted since has fully atoned for the first mistake, and left Theodore entirely without excuse for the course of conduct in which he still persists. We may, and perhaps we ought, to take into consideration the evil influences surrounding the king, in the persons of selfish foreign adventurers and unprincipled courtiers, whose crafty insinuations have continually thrown the question back again, and rendered abortive the efforts we have made to bring things to an amicable settlement ; but when we have allowed for all this, the conduct of the king in still holding our countrymen against the recognised laws of nations is quite inexcusable. Whatever argument may be found in these circumstances for after leniency towards him, no reason can be founded thereon for leaving the servants and subjects of her Majesty to the capricious pleasure of this self-willed despot. By the course we have hitherto adopted in the matter, we have in the eyes of the ignorant multitudes of Oriental nations lost a good deal of our prestige. The *hajjis* who congregate from all parts of the East to the holy city of Mecca, have got to know on arriving in the confines of the Red Sea that the black sultan of Habesh has now held for four years in chains the pale-faced subjects of " Victoria, Queen." From Jeddah to the wall of China, and from Cape Guardafui to the Gold Coast, the fact is notorious, and is the subject of remark in the khan of the Tartar and at the " palaver " of the negro. And if this state of things were permitted to continue, the nations of India would soon learn to throw off their allegiance, and the Englishmen, who for the next twenty years will be seeking the sources of the Nile, would step into foot-chains wherever they went. This must not be. The national character must be maintained, the national honour vindicated, though it cost much treasure, and even blood.

Having once decided to compel Theodore by force to relinquish his prisoners, the next question is, How can we best attain the object we have in view ? Some, like Sir Henry Bulwer and Sir Samuel Baker, recommend a joint action on the part of England and Egypt; and it may be well just for a moment to look at the probable result of such a course. Sir Henry Bulwer, in a recent letter to the *Pall Mall Gazette*, says, " With a moderate British and Sepoy force, and such assistance as the Viceroy of Egypt told me he would be ready to give, it would be no rash engagement to undertake to hang Theodorus in the chains that now torture the limbs of his captives."

We need not here stop to examine the question as to the likelihood of the British army ever having the chance (satisfaction, it may be) of seeing Theodore suspended between heaven and earth from the boughs of a " kosso " tree. The old proverb, " First catch your hare," is certainly very applicable in this case. But we will suppose that the small British and Sepoy force shall advance from the coast direct to Debra Tabor or Magdala, while the Egyptians would cross the frontier on the west, say at Matammah, and so make for the common centre. What would be the probable result of this joint action on the mind of the Abyssinian nation? Though we expressed our intention of only punishing Theodore, would the people, seeing the Turks in their country, believe that this was our only object, and still give us a free passage, and supply the necessary provisions? The mere supposition is out of the question. So intense is the hatred of Christian Abyssinia to their traditional enemies the Turks, that the possibility of an Egyptian as well as English invasion would do what Theodore failed to do—unite the whole nation as one man, and place immediately in arms every fighting man in the country, a force of well-nigh 200,000 men. Nothing would please Theodore better than such an event, for his known animosity to the Turks, and his early experience of them, would be not unlikely to ensure him the generalship of the whole army, and thus enable him to regain the position he has already lost.

It is true that we need not despair even then of accomplishing our object, but the campaign would certainly assume proportions which is not now dreamt of.

It may be urged in objection to this view, that if the Abyssinian nation would unite to resist us when joined with the "Turks," they will do the same when only an English army is concerned. I do not think it would be the case, for here the element of religious antagonism is wanting. Religion is a far more powerful motive with an Abyssinian than love of country. The testimony of Consul Plowden is very valuable on this point. He says:

"To a foreign conquest little resistance would be offered; they are too imaginative to dream of patriotism."

But he adds, "This spirit, which is entirely wanting, was supplied in their contests with the Mohammedans by fanatical excitement."

In undertaking the expedition alone therefore, though we may have occasional brushes with the partisans of different chiefs, we shall not be likely to find a united nation to oppose us. They will be very jealous of our entrance, and suspect our intentions, but the elements of discord are too great in the country to make them unite for other than a religious war.

Another point for consideration regarding an alliance

with Egypt is, that we could not expect the viceroy to aid us without consenting to allow him some compensation for the service thus rendered, and there is little doubt that the stipulation would be for permission to annex to his dominions in the Soudan some of the rich provinces of Abyssinia. Knowing Egyptian policy in the Soudan, and with the recent disclosures on the White Nile trade still fresh in memory, are we prepared for this? Are we willing to allow Abyssinia to become a rich *Christian slave mine*, to be worked as the countries on the White River are worked?

It is true that the Pasha of Egypt has lately in Paris proclaimed what would appear to be strong anti-slavery views, and has even asserted that the slave trade on that river is entirely kept up by the Europeans there engaged in it. Are we to be blinded by this assertion, made, one can well imagine, with the simple object of saying something to please his entertainers for the time being? That the viceroy's assertion is really not true is borne out by thousands of facts which cannot be impugned. For an instance of the real policy of Egypt in the Soudan, and with regard to Abyssinia, I will give here an extract from a daily paper (the *Pall Mall Gazette*) professing to furnish the latest news from those regions. The information it contains was submitted to the correspondent of the journal by a native Mohammedan Abyssinian, who had just arrived from his own country :

"A war had been going on for some time between the Abyssinian province of Shire and adjacent parts of the north-west of Tigre and the Beni Amer Arabs, who occupy the country between Shire and Waldabba on the south, and Taka on the north. The Tigreans were the aggressors [?], and had beaten the Arabs in two fights, when they resolved to attack them again on a more effective scale. The engagement came off in December last, near Baaza, to the discomfiture of the Tigreans, who were defeated with great slaughter. Of the whole Tigrean force, numbering many thousands, and attended by the women and children belonging to its members, only 200 horsemen are said to have escaped. The Tigrean force consisted chiefly of Shire people, commanded by Dejage Adik, an officer of Theodorus. The Beni Amer killed the old and useless prisoners; the younger of both sexes and children they took in triumph to Taka, the seat of the Egyptian governor of those parts, who is related to have told the

Arabs that, 'as God had given the booty into their hands, they were at liberty to dispose of it.' Accordingly, the captives were sent to market in such numbers that Christian slaves are reported to be comparatively cheap in the Red Sea ports and on the Egyptian frontier ever since."

Does this look like the dying out of the slave trade? And here surely no blame can be thrown on Europeans, as in those parts there are none existing. Let us not therefore be deceived; for, however much the viceroy himself might wish for the overthrow of this abominable traffic, those under him, especially when at such a distance from the seat of Government, will ever lend their encouragement to it, seeing the source of wealth it is to them.

However, the general tendency of opinion appears to be that, inasmuch as the quarrel is our own, we should settle it ourselves, without seeking to lighten our difficulties by appealing for aid from any other power. We may now, therefore, consider the probability of the success which would attend our own individual efforts for the liberation of the unfortunate captives. Before doing this, it is first desirable to understand the present state of the country about to become the scene of our efforts.

It is not at all improbable that the slight given by our Government to Theodore in refusing to admit him among the brotherhood of princes gave encouragement to those insurgent chiefs who have since rebelled against him, and has thus proved an indirect cause of his crippled power. Be this as it may, the revolt of the main portion of his empire may be dated from the time of our refusal to recognise him being made known.

In the autumn of 1863 an insurrection took place in Tigre under a chief of the name of Kassa Goldja, who seized the country between the Mareb and Tecazze, and afterwards made a descent on Adowa. His attack was repulsed, and he was obliged to retreat, but he was still powerful enough to give a good deal of trouble, by making frequent raids on the territory subject to the governor of Tigre, appointed by Theodore.

Kassa Goldja's revolt was immediately succeeded by the rebellion of Tessu Góbasie, a native of Waldabba, and formerly a general of Oubie's. This chief seized upon the provinces of Waldabba, Walkait, Armatjoho, Woggera, and Simyen, and even pursued his ravages into Dembea to Gondar, the capital. He also attacked and killed Mek Amer, son of the Mek Nimr who burnt alive Ismail Pasha in 1827, and afterwards fled for protection to the Abyssinian border. Mek Amer was an ally of Theodore, and very troublesome to the Turks, upon whose territory he made frequent inroads, and it was no doubt with the idea of conciliating the latter that Tessu dealt thus summarily with the Arab chief. He is also said to have accused Mek Amer of being the cause of the imprisonment of our countrymen, though in what way this can have been it is difficult to determine. A possible explanation may be, that Amer communicated certain false reports to Theodore, concerning Captain Cameron's journey through the Egyptian territory, on the strength of which the king withdrew his favour from our consul, but we know that Captain Cameron's imprisonment was due to the mistake of our Government, and to that only. Amer had previously shown himself favourable to our countrymen, in the persons of Mansfield Parkyns, and (I believe) Sir Samuel Baker; and why he should have formed a different opinion of Captain Cameron it is hard to say.

The insurrection of Tessu was followed by the uprising of Shoa, the inhabitants of which rallied round Menilek, the son of their former king, who had escaped

U

by flight from Theodore's camp; and this large province of the empire was again rendered independent. Hither the king hurried with his army, but being attacked on the road by the Wollo Gallas, also in revolt, his expedition failed, and he was obliged to make a hasty retreat.

Encouraged by the success of the other insurgents, Tadla Gualoo of Gojam also made inroads into Theodore's territory, regaining his mountain fortress with the booty thus obtained.

But the most formidable revolt of all was that of Waagshum Góbasie, Prince of Lasta, who succeeded in investing himself of the whole of Eastern Abyssinia, with the exception of a few provinces to the north. He is said by Dr. Beke to lay claim to the throne of all Abyssinia, and to be about to follow the example of the king in adopting the name of Hezekiah, to fulfil a prophecy which points to a monarch of that name, who is to precede the true Theodore. The fashion of forcing prophecy is not very logical, and, though it almost succeeded with the Abyssinian nation in the case of Theodore, it is not very likely it will take a second time. Góbasie, perhaps, has a notion of ridiculing Theodore by imitating him.

Later accounts report a division in the force of the latter, a brother, or near relation of his, of the name of Kassu, having revolted and taken with him a considerable portion of his army. This is the same old story—rebellion within rebellion, every man's hand against his brother. A little longer, and the unfortunate nation will have destroyed itself, unless the foreigner come first and rule their country for them.

From the above, it will be seen, on a reference to the map, that the territory now left to Theodore consists of little more than a strip of land round Lake Tsana, embracing the provinces of Begemeder (as far as Magdala), Bellesa, Dembea, Tchelga, Dagossa, Kuara, Mietcha, and part of Gojam. The governors of Adowa, Shire, and Hamaseyn, are also said to be faithful to him, though they are unable to render him any very active service. The provinces above-mentioned certainly include the richest and most fertile portion of Abyssinia, and so long as these remain faithful to him, he will have little to fear from the isolated attacks of any of the other insurgent chiefs. But, if recent accounts are true, his hold even upon these parts is very slender, and the attachment of the people is more the result of fear than of devotion.

Frequent desertions have also reduced his army to a number said not to exceed 5000. This estimate is that of the captives themselves, but we must receive it with caution. Pent up in Magdala, they are not in a good position to ascertain exactly the real extent of the king's force. Some of them maintained six months since that he had but so many troops left, and yet they have subsequently spoken of wholesale desertions amounting fully to that number. Five thousand, however, is their latest account specified.

And now, what is likely to be the policy of King Theodore, when he hears of our determination to attack him? At present, he is at Debra Tabor, his capital, where he is invariably in the habit of spending the rainy season. In the month of October, on the termination of the rains, he will be able to move about within his limited territory wherever he likes; and, as long before October he will have heard of our preparations, what are likely to be his tactics in the face of this new danger?

If is, of course, mere matter for speculation. I will state what I think.

In my opinion, he will first have recourse to stratagem. He will seem to temporise. Before we enter

the country we may expect him to write smooth letters
to the commander-in-chief of our army, in which he will
dwell on the friendship previously existing between
the two nations; declaring that he never wished it to
have been broken: how he welcomed Rassam, when
he was sent to re-establish it, and detained him merely
with the idea of "consulting further on the extension
of it." He will then get Mr. Rassam to write pretty
much at his dictation, corroborating all that he himself had said, and praying that no offensive course
should be taken. Further epistles will be sent both
from the king and Mr. Rassam (whom the king, by acting on his fears, will think to make a tool of), the object
of which will be, though done in as sly and crafty way
as possible, to get us to assist him in reconquering
his country, on the condition of his liberating the captives. During these negotiations, he will also try, by
various pretences (but all on the " Will you walk into
my parlour ?" principle), to get some influential men on
the expedition to visit him at his court, and he will
also seek by these means to gain time until the
approach of another rainy season shall compel us for
the time to desist from our enterprise. Notwithstanding
all these shifts, he will certainly find himself circum-

vented; for Mr. Rassam has already proved to be a match for him, though the king does not know it, he having arranged that by certain signs in the letters themselves we may know when they have been written at his Ethiopic Majesty's dictation. Moreover, it is scarcely likely that the officers in charge of the expedition will be in this way deceived. There are propositions which we ourselves will certainly make, but they will be based on the immediate surrender of the captives, if not on a proper compensation for their detention as well.

These negotiations having fallen through, what will be the king's next step? Will he give us battle? This is not likely. If the reports of the captives themselves are true, he only possesses a force of 5000; at any rate, he wields a diminished force; and as he, more than any other chief in the country, knows the advantages of discipline in an army (he has indeed made some ineffectual attempts to establish it in his own), he will never dare to put that number of unskilled men in the field against the force we should bring against him.

Will he retire to Magdala, and make his stand there?

This supposition is scarcely more likely than the other. From experience gained in contests with the

Egyptian troops on his western frontiers, and from the instructions of Bell and Plowden, his two English generals, the king knows as well as we do that to attempt to hold his mountain fortress against European war appliances would be hopeless, suicidal to him and his cause. Have not all the plans for the construction of mortars and cannon in his own country, which have engaged his attention for the last ten years, been based on his knowledge of the superiority of Europe in these matters? And was it not with the idea of dislodging by these means, Tadla Gualoo, Governor of Gojam, from his mountain fort of Djibella (the exact counterpart of Magdala), that he had his mortars constructed? Surely Theodore is not the fool some would take him to be. However invulnerable against native war appliances, he would never attempt to hold Magdala against a British army.

Nor is it probable that he will leave the captives there and keep himself out of the way. If he is inclined to give the captives up at all he will do so before our entry into the country, at the instance of our ulti-matum, rather than wait for our entrance to induce his compliance.

None of the above courses do I think the king will

take. The greater probability is that he will disband his soldiers for the time being, sending them on our track as spies, with secret orders to unite in small bands and harass our rear, or cut off our supplies, if such an opportunity should offer; while he himself, with a small company and the captives, will retire into the mountain fastnesses of his native Kuara. *He may even determine not to be burdened at all with the captives,* and, however we may shudder at the thought of that dread contingency, we are solemnly bound to take it into our consideration. My reason for conceiving that the king will retire into Kuara, is that Kuara is his native province; the rule of it has always been in his family; he will there feel more secure against capture or betrayal. Moreover, having spent his youth there, he knows every nook and cranny of the province. This supposition is also borne out by the fact that, whenever in his previous history, before becoming king, his life was hard pressed by the other chiefs of the country, he always sought a safe retreat in his native province. When, as a youth, he escaped from the convent besieged by Dejage Maro, he fled to Kuara. When afterwards, as warrior-chief, he was defeated by Birru Goshu, Governor of Gojam, he found a refuge here, and remained in his retreat a whole twelvemonth, unknown even to his friends. On another occasion, even when his own province was occupied by the enemy, he evaded their vigilance by living disguised in a peasant's hut. If therefore his knowledge of the mountain passes and secret places of his own province sufficed to shield him from the Abyssinians themselves, how difficult will it be for the British army to catch him! He is aware of it, and therefore his policy will be by false reports to keep us running over the country after him until we are thoroughly tired out. And, in my opinion, Tantia Topee and Nana Sahib were tyros in the art of eluding disciplined troops compared with the crafty and agile Theodore. Should he, however, in any way be hard pressed by us, rather than fall into our hands, he would certainly put an end to his own life.

III. Comparison of the Practicable Routes for a Military Expedition to Central Abyssinia.—And now as to the expedition. As a summary of what is generally known on this point, I here give an extract from a daily paper which professes to have " taken some trouble to glean the information from trustworthy sources." The *Daily Telegraph* of the 14th of September says :—" The resolve of the public is, that we must rescue our compatriots from the treacherous captor ; the expectation is, that the means devoted to the task shall be so thoroughly efficient as to command success. Hence the scale of the preparations. The invading army is to be made up of 10,000 troops, chiefly Punjaubees, and a proportion of cavalry. An Indian army cannot move without an immense train of attendants ; and accordingly, at the lowest estimate, the camp-followers must be set down at no fewer than 25,000, from the wild Lascar to the ' ferocious Dhoolie.' With these are to be sent four field batteries of artillery, and also one mountain battery, consisting of six rifled steel seven-pounder guns, which are to be carried on mules. Next, there is to be a supply of Hale's rockets, 5000 breech-loaders and revolvers, and a field telegraph. Such an army cannot move without a vast number of beasts of burden, and hence there are to be 21,000 mules and 5000 camels. So much for the actual invasion of Abyssinia."

The expedition will be placed under the command of Sir Robert Napier, who is to be entrusted with the chief political as well as military authority.

There are several routes by which Theodore's territory can be reached. Let us briefly consider them.

1st. The route *viâ* TAJOURA. Tajoura, lying on the African coast, just without the Straits of Bâb el-Mandeb, is seven days' steaming from Bombay. The port is bad, and there is little convenience for the landing of troops. The distance to Magdala is about 400 miles;* to Debra Tabor, 500. The first part of the route, through the Adal desert to the foot of the Abyssinian table-land, is tolerably even, but very hot and unhealthy, with a great scarcity of water, except where the river Hawash is followed. The remaining portion is very rough, though healthy, and affording abundance of pure water and forage. The tribes we have to pass through on this road are the Adaiel, a wandering people, savage and treacherous, but not numerous; and the Wollo Gallas, wild and brave horsemen, but who, having a grudge against Theodore, might chance to be friendly. The English general has the opportunity of propitiating them.

2nd. The route from RAHEITA, just within the straits of Bâb el-Mandeb, in every respect similar to the preceding one, but a little shorter.

3rd. The route from AMPHILA, through the territory

* The figures here given represent approximate distances by road.

of the TALTALS, and AZUBO GALLAS, to the neighbourhood of LAKE ASHANGI, and so over the Abyssinian
highlands to Magdala or Debra Tabor. Distance to
Magdala, 400 miles; to Debra Tabor the same. The
Taltals are a barbarous and bloodthirsty race, but not
numerous. Their country is undulating, and covered
with herbage for the cattle, but there is a scarcity of
water. The Azubo Gallas are, like all their race, brave
but cruel, moderately numerous, and their country well-
watered and fertile. Thence the province of Lasta
is entered by steep mountain passes. The country is
fertile, cool and healthy, but the roads are rather rough.
This province is the territory of Waagshum Góbasie, who
offered some time since to liberate the captives for us on
condition of our supporting him in his claim to the
throne of Abyssinia. He might be friendly if we com-
plied with these conditions; otherwise he would put
obstacles in our way to the extent of his power, and it
would be for the discretion of General Napier to consider the policy of treating with him. The remaining
portion of the route through Angot and Dalanta is in
the hands of Gallas and Amharas, who could offer no
resistance. They having just thrown off allegiance to
Theodore, might help us by furnishing provisions, &c.

The route from Lasta direct to Debra Tabor would be through territory nominally in subjection to Theodore.

4th. The route from AMPHILA direct on to the Abyssinian table-land at ATEGERAT, and thence through Lasta to Theodore's territory. It is similar to the preceding, but offers more of cool, healthy country, though it is more rugged. One or other of these routes has been much thought of lately, but now we believe relinquished. Amphila has a good port, according to Colonel Merewether.

5th. The route from ZULLAH at the bottom of Annesley Bay on to the highlands at Halai, and thence through Tigre proper and Lasta to Magdala, or through Tigre and Simyen, Minna and Bellesa, to Debra Tabor. Magdala, 400 miles; Debra Tabor, the same. This is the most healthy of all, as the cool table-land is reached in two days. It is, however, at least in its approaches, the most rugged. If our object should be to reach Magdala, the road would branch off in the neighbourhood of Tembyen, proceeding thence through Lasta, as by the two former routes. If we are aiming at Debra Tabor, the most direct is the one described in the 11th and 12th chapters of the Narrative, viz. *viâ* Halai, Adowa, Tembyen, the valley of the Tecazze, Bellesa, and Ebenat. As it is thought in some quarters that the country will be entered in this direction, I shall make some more extended remarks on this route afterwards.

6th. The route from MASSOWAH, through Hamaseyn to Adowa, and so on, as by the foregoing, to Debra Tabor or Magdala. Distance to both places about 420 miles. Four or five days would be required by the army to reach the cool highlands by this road, but it is by no means so rough as that *viâ* Halai. The Governor of Hamaseyn is still faithful to Theodore, but could not offer the least resistance. Hamaseyn passed, Tigre is entered, and the road to Adowa is moderately easy. From Adowa as in previous route.

7th. The route from MASSOWAH, *viâ* BOGOS, KASSALA, and MATAMMAH, to Debra Tabor or Magdala. Very circuitous, but has very many advantages notwithstanding. The distance about 600 miles to Debra Tabor, 700 to Magdala. The territory as far as Matammah is almost entirely in the possession of Egypt, and at Matammah Theodore's territory is entered immediately. No insurgent chiefs to treat with. The whole route can be traversed by camels, and supplies would be abundant. Water plentiful, and forage for cattle. The first half of the journey is healthy, but the second, from Kassala to Matammah, is hot, and subject to malaria. On leaving Matammah the healthy highlands are reached, which continue the remainder of the journey.

8th. The route from SOUAKIM to KASSALA and MATAMMAH, and so to Debra Tabor or Magdala. This is similar to the preceding as far as distance is concerned, but the time taken in the journey might be made even less than the others, at least to Debra Tabor. This route has the best advantages for the march of an army, as the country traversed is for the most part flat and open. The whole distance can be done by camels, which would find abundance of fodder. Supplies are abundant when the district of Taka is entered. Water plentiful, except for the first hundred miles. Unhealthy between Kassala and Matammah. The tribes occupying the road tributary to Egypt, and so would be friendly. Debra Tabor, 600 miles; Magdala, 700. I shall have more to say about this road afterwards.

The above are, I believe, all the routes which have been mentioned in connection with this subject, as, indeed, they are the only ones at all practicable by which this mountainous country can be entered. The route which it is generally believed the expedition will take is one of those leading to the highlands direct from Massowah. I say this is generally believed to be the case; but the adoption of any one of them is doubtful, for the objections are many and imperative, as we will endeavour to prove.

The probability is, that on Theodore's hearing of our intention to attack him, he will, at the cessation of the rains, have the prisoners brought down from Magdala to Debra Tabor, so as to be ready, if hard pressed, to retreat with them towards Kuara. In that event, at the time our expedition is ready to start (December), Debra Tabor will be the spot towards which we shall have to make; consequently, the nearest route from Massowah to Debra Tabor will at first sight present itself as the one which ought to be taken. Now, if the reader will look at the map placed in the front of this book, he will see that, without doubt, the most direct road from Massowah to Debra Tabor is the one I myself traversed, there marked with a red tracing. This will especially be found to be the case if it is supposed, as would be probable, that the troops are landed near Zulla, in Annesley Bay. We may, therefore, consider that the army would have to follow from north-east to south-west the identical road I traversed from south-west to north-east; consequently, a few remarks on the nature of this route may not be unprofitable.

In the first place, the troops on landing would have a plain of some ten miles in extent to cross before the foot of the Taranta mountain is reached. The line would be mostly over the sands, which swallow up during the greater part of the year the mountain torrent called the Hadas. Water, however, could easily be obtained by digging a few feet, as I have related was done by my Shoho guide. This tract crossed, the mountains now begin to close in on each side, and you pass up a narrow defile, without opening to the right or left, until the summit of the pass is reached. The mountains on each side are almost inaccessible, save to goats and bare-footed Shohos: they attain, at the commencement of the route, a height above the bed of the Hadas of at least 1000 feet. The breadth of this defile averages some twenty or thirty yards, but the bottom is so covered with angular rocks and boulders, that you are almost compelled to go single file. Indeed, the nature of the pass would enable 500 well-armed, resolute Abyssinians to hold it against an army, the rocks and trees forming an excellent ambush.

x

As the territory, however, is only occupied by Shohos, who do not possess guns and are not numerous, no obstacle would be found but in the nature of the road itself. Bruce has described it so accurately (and its quality may also be gathered by the account I have given of my descent of it), that nothing more need be said. It will be a work of toil, tasking the endurance and spirit of our men severely.

It must not be concluded that all difficulties are overcome when once the table-land is reached. A few hours from Halai the army will have to descend again, and by an abrupt and rugged descent too, though nothing like the Taranta. We now reach a plain covered with thorny trees and rough sharp-cornered boulders, which continues, though on a gradual incline, till the valley of the Mareb is reached. The Mareb is easily crossed, having at this time (December) but one or two feet of water; and then succeeds a low flat plain, where the heat is rather great, but not excessively so. There is also a breath of malaria hanging about here, but an ordinary traveller passes the infested district in a few hours, and the army might do it in a day. We now begin gradually to ascend again until we arrive at the summit of a perfectly flat plateau, cool and healthy, which continues for a few miles, after which another descent is made, rugged, but not steep, and, the valley succeeding it being crossed, begin to ascend again on to a plateau similar to the last. Several in fact have to be crossed until Adowa is reached, at about one hundred miles from Halai. Adowa lies rather low, but not so much so as the Mareb; consequently while the neigh-bourhood is rather warm it is comparatively healthy.

On leaving Adowa a plain road is traversed for some time, but then succeed several ridges of high hills covered with boulders and thorny trees, where the path is sometimes so narrow that the army would have to go single file. One passes sometimes also along the sides of mountains, whose incline is so great that a false step would endanger the lives of mule and rider. These animals, however, can be depended upon. Footmen stand a better chance without shoes than with, and would thus be able to proceed in safety. Some fifty miles over these rocky hills brings one to Tembyen (Abiyad), in a rich and fertile valley, lying probably on a level with Adowa. The sun here is hot. Tembyen is a thriving Mohammedan town; supplies to a limited extent might be got here.

On leaving Tembyen the River Gevha is soon after

reached, but the road throughout is unpleasant, both to mules and men. The path continues for some time along the bed of the Gevha, a mountain stream, shallow and narrow ; and then branches off direct to the Tecazze over a rough country of slaty formation. The Tecazze is about seventy miles from Adowa, and runs in a deep rocky ravine, with precipitous sides, where it is hot, but, owing to the want of vegetation, not unhealthy. The road continues along the bed of the Tecazze for another fifty miles, during which the stream itself is crossed every two or three miles. It was practicable enough when I passed it at the end of the dry season, but may be more difficult in the month of January, when our troops would have to pass it. It would then probably have some three feet of water.

On leaving the Tecazze the route is excessively rugged and tortuous, passing over spurs of the Simyen mountains, whose summits are covered with snow. But the air here is cool and pleasant, enabling one to bear better the excessive fatigue. Forty miles from the Tecazze the River Minna is reached, a tributary of the Tecazze, and not much inferior in volume of water to that stream itself. Unlike the Tecazze, its banks are clothed with rich foliage, including monster tamarind and sycamore trees, whose shade at noon is delightful. The Minna is some hundred feet broad.

On quitting the Minna the road crosses in succession mountain after mountain, covered with wood and shattered fragments of rock, for a distance of fifty miles or so. We find that we have then attained the vast plain of Bellesa, perfectly even, but dotted here and there with flat-topped rocks, the remains of the original plateau. Some thirty miles along this plain brings us to the eastern foot of Mount Melza, and by a short and abrupt ascent we attain a small plain beneath its highest summit, in which stands the large village of Ebenat. Crossing the plain of Ebenat, a rough descent carries us into the rocky Reb valley, and a similar ascent on the other side to the undulating plain, at the farther extremity of which stands Gaffat, with Debra Tabor town and mountain presiding above.*

The time taken by me in traversing the distance was twenty-one days, not including stoppages; and as I averaged about twenty miles a day, the distance from Massowah to Debra Tabor is in round numbers 400 miles. But the march of an army is a vastly different

* The description of this road was given in a letter to the *Times* of the 14th of September.

thing to the journey of a private traveller, possessed as
I was of a good ambling mule. In India the average
distance traversed by an army in a day is about ten
miles. Now the routes in India, in those parts where
our troops have been most engaged, may, I think, be
said to be less difficult than the Abyssinian; indeed an
Abyssinian road, even the most frequented, is nothing
better than a sheep track, except in and around Debra
Tabor, where Theodore has lately experimented in mac-
adamizing. We may reasonably conclude, therefore,
that ten miles will be the utmost extent of what our
army will get through per diem, and that consequently
the march from the coast to the king's capital will
occupy at least forty days. This is easily to be believed
when it is considered that the army will in very many
instances have to march single file.

But is not this last circumstance, namely, the strag-
gling nature of the march, a very potent objection against
this route altogether? If the people on the line of
march are inclined to be adverse to us, have they not,
with their knowledge of the mountain passes and by-
paths of their country, a means thus put into their hands
of doing us an immense deal of injury? A few hundred
of them might with little difficulty break the connection

between the different portions of the army, capture a gun, or stop the road by hurling vast masses of rock down from above. Such stratagems are the peculiar forte of the Abyssinian.

But it has been urged that, as the insurgent chiefs who occupy the territory through which we shall pass are opposed to Theodore, we might expect them to be friendly to ourselves. This is a great mistake. In Abyssinia the hand of everyone is against his brother; and if they are thus quarrelsome amongst themselves, we cannot reasonably imagine that they will be permanently faithful to foreigners. The Abyssinian, knowing that all the countries round about him are mostly sterile deserts, is apt, in his ignorance, to believe that the rest of the world is pretty much in the same condition, and so thinks that his own beautiful country is the object of admiration and desire to all foreign nations. That Egypt covets it he knows, and he will think that England on seeing it will do the same. Almost all he has heard about England is that she has conquered and held India, and he believes that conquest is therefore our policy. We may tell him as much as we like that our only object is the liberation of our countrymen, but we shall never persuade him that an army of 12,000

men (he will see 50,000 even in our vast host) is sent
for the purpose of rescuing a few prisoners. It will be
a thing totally incomprehensible to him that we march
that army into Abyssinia simply to vindicate our national
honour. In his eyes our entrance will be an invasion,
with the object of making Abyssinia another India. He
will consequently resist us as far as he is able, not
unitedly, but individually, by withholding supplies and
beasts of burden. We need not reckon on getting from
him a solitary cow or bushel of corn, or a mule to carry
our baggage. The resistance of individual chiefs and
their partisans we may also expect, especially if we
choose any one like Waagshum Góbasie, and favour his
claims, for by this means we should only excite the
animosity of the others; and there are five of these, let-
ting alone Theodore, who are almost as powerful as the
Waagshum.

We may also expect that the whole nation will be on
the alert after plunder, for they will see in the baggage
and accoutrements of our army what will enrich the
country to the end of the present century, and give it a
power and position in Africa which it would otherwise
never attain.

Then comes the question, How are we to keep open

communication with the coast for the conveyance of despatches, the renewal of supplies, or for reinforcements in case of need ? The last, it is to be hoped, we shall not require. Fresh supplies from the coast we certainly shall want, unless enough are taken in the first instance to last the whole campaign. But as we have not the remotest idea how long the campaign itself will last, we cannot say what quantity of provisions would be required. Nor can we depend upon the country itself; that much is certain. We must, therefore, for this reason only, preserve some means of communication with the coast. So, also, for the conveyance of despatches. It has been suggested that we should have a line of telegraph laid down in the track of the army ; but although the abundance of trees offers every advantage for the purpose, yet the inhabitants would assuredly destroy it immediately. We must depend upon messengers, and these would require a large escort for their safe passage. So we shall be compelled to leave a force at different points on the route, by means of which the road may be kept open. The most likely places for such detachments would be Halai, Adowa, and some spot on the Tecazze. But what force would be required at each place to guard against attack ? A thousand I do not think would suffice,

for either Waagshum Góbasie or Tessu could raise at
any time an army of 20,000 ; and, notwithstanding European superiority, with twenty to one the odds would
press heavily against us.   We cannot reckon otherwise
than that a large portion of our army is at once withdrawn, merely for the sake of keeping open communication with the coast.

Another objection to the route, and one deserving our
serious consideration, is the following :—There is, as I
have already remarked, a dreadful possibility, which,
however heart-chilling the very thought of it may be to
us, we are nevertheless imperatively bound not to close
our eyes to, that Theodore, in a fit of rage and de-
speration, may, on hearing of our having entered his
country for the purpose of attacking him, give the order
to have all the Europeans in his possession mercilessly
slaughtered.   In view of this awful contingency, it is
highly desirable that no efforts should be lost by means
of parley or negotiation to obtain the liberation of our
countrymen before we adopt any stronger measures.
Now, Massowah is by no means the place from which
such negotiations can be made.   The distance is so great
from Theodore's territory, and the means of communication, being through an adverse country, so uncertain,

that the only time allowed for the expedition to act with safety in (December to May) might in this manner be frittered away, and nothing be done in the end. And if we enter Abyssinia in this direction with the idea of getting nearer to Theodore before making the propositions we may have to make, we may be met on the way by the news that the objects of our solicitude are no more. So unyielding and tenacious is Theodore to the right he maintains over the whole of Abyssinia, that if we only reach with our army the frontier village of Halai, he will take this as an invasion of his territory, and act accordingly. Our object, therefore, should be to get to that portion of the Abyssinian frontier which is nearest to his capital, and from which communications can the most easily be made. Now, there is only one spot where it can be done; and, by what may be regarded as a fortunate concurrence of circumstances, this happens to be on one of the two high roads to Abyssinia. Massowah is the main approach to Abyssinia on the east, Matammah on the north; and the last is, in my opinion, the road, and only road, by which we should approach Theodore. From the frontier near Matammah a messenger can reach Theodore at Debra Tabor in five days, and would pass through territory that has always acknowledged his sway; whereas from Massowah a messenger could not do it in less than fifteen, and then he would have to run the gauntlet of all the insurgent chiefs. Not only so: for the sake of negotiation Theodore might approach to within a few miles of his frontier in this direction, and thus render parley more easy; but he cannot stir at all in the direction of Massowah, by reason of the rebel chiefs. I think, therefore, that Matammah is the safest and best spot whence these preliminary negotiations can be directed. They may possibly lead to the release of the prisoners without a blow being struck; but if not, we shall be enabled to say that we have done our best, and that their blood, if it be shed, will rest on the head of the despot alone.

But, quite apart from these considerations, the Matammah route has in itself many other advantages over all the others, as I will endeavour to make clear. There are two routes by which Matammah can be approached from the Red Sea: one by way of Massowah, Keren in Bogos, Kassala and Gedárif; the second from Souakim direct to Kassala and Gedárif. Of these two, I think on the whole the second is preferable, as being the most direct, and running through an open plain country, well adapted for the march of an army, whereas the other, at the beginning of the route, namely, from Massowah to Kassala, is mountainous, and consequently rough. It is somewhat pleasanter, however, not being so hot, and passing through fine scenery, and só may be adopted by those on the expedition whose presence is not absolutely required in the army—the geographical and scientific portion, for instance, if such be attached.

There have been many objections made to the Souakim road, and these it may be as well to dispose of first. The principal and most obvious one, and the one which I am afraid has caused it to be put altogether aside, is its distance from the scene of operations. Now, if it be assumed (and this, I believe, is the prevalent idea) that the Abyssinian question is to be settled at Magdala, I will admit that the length of the journey is a potent objection, though even then not sufficient to throw in the shade the other positive and striking advantages distinguishing it. But I have already expressed my opinion—it amounts in this case almost to a moral certainty—that Theodore will not make his stand at Magdala, and that his native province of Kuara is the part to which he is most likely ultimately to retire.

Should my view be correct, the objection on the ground of distance is quite done away with; for, considering the sinuosities of the Massowah route compared with the straight course of the Souakim, there would be little to choose between them. Both roads to the centre of the province of Kuara would be about 600 miles. But here another point must be taken into consideration, and that is the time which would be taken in the two journeys respectively. I have before stated my opinion, grounded on the marches of our troops in India, that ten miles will be the limit of the army's march per diem. The consequence is, that if Theodore should withdraw into Kuara, the march from the coast into that district will occupy two months—rather a serious affair for an army. Now let us take the Souàkim road. Here we have an uninterrupted plain path with not a solitary hill of any importance all the way from Souakim to Matammah; and if ten miles is reckoned as a day's work in Abyssinia, fifteen miles is surely not too high a figure to be attached to the road now proposed. Reckoning the distance, therefore, as 600 miles to Kuara, the whole journey may be accomplished in forty days, two-thirds only of what that viâ Massowah would require. That my calculation is an accurate one I would here seek to establish by calling in the testimony of Sir Samuel Baker. In a recent letter to the *Times* that experienced traveller says, that the army of Giaffer Pasha, sent into the Soudan in 1865, took just twenty days of slow marching in the journey from Souakim to Kassala. A glance at the map will show at once that Kassala is exactly half way to Kuara; consequently the remaining portion of the road, even allowing for a little roughness from Matammah to that province, need not take more than twenty to twenty-five days. So much for the objection on the score of distance.

The second objection to the Souakim route is its unhealthiness. Now, I believe this point has been unduly magnified. The first part of the journey from Souakim to near Kassala is by no means unhealthy, the road lying through a tract perfectly dry, and being totally free from the rank, malaria-engendering vegetation which marks the remainder of the road as far as Matammah. The latter half of the route, therefore, is the only dangerous part; and this, which is estimated in the country as a six-days' camel ride, would very well be accomplished in twelve days by the army. If proper sanatory precautions are taken, disease may be warded off. It must be remembered also that intermittent fever, which is the disease, and only one, to be feared, is not at all dangerous, and disappears immediately the Abyssinian highlands are reached.

Another objection raised to this route is the alleged want of water from Souakim to near Kassala. I admit that for a space of six months there is drought along this road, but when we bear in mind that our army will have to pass it soon after the rainy season, the objection is answered. It is well known that a branch of the Atbara has a course in the rainy season half way from Kassala to Souakim, and being then swallowed up by the sands, the water is still attainable by digging for almost the whole of the remaining distance. Dr. Beke mentions some French travellers who really saw the branch stream. at that season disembogue into the Red Sea. Admitting, however, that this is not an annual phenomenon, sinking of a well here and there through a few feet of sand will certainly be no great task on the engineering skill of the sappers and miners, which department for many other reasons will have to be pretty well represented in the army. Taking even the worst aspect of the case, that water must be carried, a few hundred more camels would obviate every difficulty.

Such are my replies to the objections to this route. I will point out its superior advantages.

The first of these—and it is one of overwhelming importance—is that only half the force proposed, 6000 instead of 12,000 men, would be requisite if Theodore's dominions are reached in this way. The Egyptian government being peculiarly interested in the weakening of Abyssinia, we may reasonably expect that the whole of the tribes on the route subject to that power, and which extend as far as Wekhni, the first village of Abyssinia, would be perfectly friendly, and render us every assistance in their power, so that there would not be the slightest occasion to leave *any* troops on the way to keep open the communication with Souakim, and thus our whole force might be employed for the object we have in view. That 6000 men are quite sufficient to conquer Theodore, were he rash enough to engage our troops, need not be doubted for a moment. Supposing the Massowah route, and not the Souakim, were chosen, we should not, after leaving a sufficient series of fortified posts in our rear to keep the road open, have really more than that number at our disposal for battle. If, therefore, we can adopt a route that will enable us to dispense with the force necessary to ensure our supplies reaching us through an adverse country, what an immense saving of life and treasure would be gained!

By the Souakim route, moreover, the project for a line of telegraph could be carried out with the greatest ease, and if carefully put up might possibly find a purchaser in the Egyptian government afterwards.

The second advantage is, that every means of transport would be abundantly furnished us. An order from the viceroy (if not the simple desire of gain) would place at our disposal 2000 or more camels, brought together from the vast camel-breeding districts of Berber, Khartoum, and Kassala. These animals traverse the whole road from Souakim right to Wekhni, Theodore's first village, a fact which I myself can witness to, they having accompanied me as far as that place. The fifty miles from Wekhni to Tchelga once passed, and notwithstanding the roughness of the way it might be done, the remaining portion of the country within a circuit of fifty miles round Lake Tsana, would be easily available to this animal. The reason the camel is not used in this portion of Abyssinia is owing more to the coolness of the climate than to anything else; but this would be little felt during a campaign of a few months, and in the dry season (November to

June). Moreover the camel, which is often yoked to the plough in Egypt, and to artillery in India, could be easily employed to the latter purpose, if required, from Souakim to Matammah. From Matammah to Tchelga the road is too rough to allow of a wheel being run over it, but the camel carries often from 5 cwt. to 6 cwt., and would easily serve to transport our guns when taken out of their carriages. Two mountain guns are a light weight for a camel.

Then, again, Matammah is the principal market on the whole of the Abyssinian frontier for horses, mules, and donkeys. If a person of some discretion had been sent forward as soon as the time allowed in our ultimatum had expired, he might have bought up any number, provided, at least, that the object for which they were intended was not allowed to transpire, otherwise Theodore would stop the export. A number of Arabs would therefore have been the most likely persons to employ for this purpose.

A third advantage is, that our army could be victualled from the country itself, instead of being dependent for supplies on India and England. The vast doura-growing and cattle-breeding districts on the Atbara and Blue Nile will supply any amount of provisions, if our messengers are despatched in time to Kassala, Gedárif, Meselemieh, and Khartoum, to lay up stores for us. Cattle, sheep, and goats are abundant here, and the country yields plentiful crops of *doura* (millet), wheat, peas, and beans. The difference in expense in this item of the commissariat alone would be immense, compared with the course of supplying the army from India.

These are the advantages which recommend the Souakim route above all others. The army should land about the beginning of October, reaching the Abyssinian frontier in the middle of November, but from the state of the preparations now being made we cannot hope to see General Napier in full activity till some two months later. As I have said above, before proceeding on to Wekhni, it would be as well to give Theodore another chance, an ultimatum absolutely requiring the liberation of the captives, and such compensation for their detention as may be deemed fit. What this is to be it is hard to say, for Theodore must be pretty nearly bankrupt now—his dollars will be scarce. His great ancestor, Solomon, once said, it was wrong to take a man's bed from under him if he couldn't pay his debts, but one really does not see what else we can get out of

Theodore except his territory. However, as his spies, which we may expect to take up on the road, will by that time have informed him of our movements, and given him all particulars as to the strength and re- sources of our army, he may possibly reconsider the matter, and so, at the eleventh hour, set the Europeans at liberty; and, perhaps, we shall be too glad to get these sixty-two poor captives safe out of his clutches to think about the compensation.

Pending a reply to our message, which might require ten days to reach us, it would not be advisable for our army to rest at Matamma, owing to its unhealthiness. Proceeding at once on to the healthy highlands, some two days' journey in advance, there would be nothing to fear. So long as we do not enter Wekhni, we cannot be said to have really invaded the country, which it would not be advisable to do before receiving a reply to our message. About half-way from Matammah to Wekhni, an admirable spot for camping-ground, secure, healthy, and with a supply of water, may be found. This is a perfectly even plain, about a mile or two in breadth, half-way up the side of a mountain, and lying on the main road from Matammah to Wekhni. Through the plain course several small rivulets of

pure cold water, nourishing sufficient timber to answer
the purpose of fuel. If Theodore's reply should be
adverse, five days would suffice to reach Tchelga,
the first place of any importance after Wekhni,
whence the army could proceed with its manœuvres in
accordance with the course adopted by the king. From
Tchelga, the whole of Theodore's dominions (except
Kuara) may be traversed by the roads which he himself has constructed; and, if our stay should be prolonged, the plains around Lake Tsana, which form the
granary of Abyssinia, can be occupied and sown—perhaps, after all, the best means of bringing Theodore to
his senses.

The latter course, namely, that of occupying Theodore's territory as the means to attain our object, will
eventually be the one which we shall have to have
recourse to, and so might as well be adopted immediately on our entering the country. If Theodore retires
(as I think he will do) to the unknown wilds to the
west or south, it would be useless to attempt to drag an
army after him through rugged mountain-passes, or low,
unhealthy tracts of jungle; and if a few regiments of
light cavalry were detached for the purpose, they would
find the enemy more than a match for them, for there

are not better horsemen in the world than the Abyssinians. Then there is all the risk of getting on a wrong scent, and no doubt Theodore will do his utmost to put us in this position. He will send numbers of his own spies to our camp, who will report that he is in such and such a place; and, the same story being repeated by a hundred different messengers, we may be inclined to believe it, and act accordingly, when, perhaps, we shall find, after a fatiguing march of some weeks, that the whole affair has been a stratagem of Theodore's. *He is even capable of coming himself to tell us where he is*, and though he were recognised by Abyssinians in our army, not one would probably dare to identify him, such is the terror in which he is held by those of his own nation; and on his return he would drop us a polite note, thanking us for the kind treatment he had received at our hands. Considering, therefore, the difficulty of catching him, I do not think it would be wise to march our army, or even a portion of it, through the fever-stricken lowlands of Kuara, when, by occupying the healthy plains round Tsana, we can accomplish our purpose much better. Why not settle down at Debra Tabor for a stay, and induce or force the peasantry to return and cultivate their fields, the produce of which, with their cattle, will support the army? If Theodore values his territory at all, this will be the most likely course to bring him to terms.

The desirability of this course will be further made clear when it is considered that we shall not in this way endanger the lives of our countrymen to the extent we should were the other course adopted. I am inclined to think the king will not immediately sacrifice his prisoners, even though we enter his country, but that he will take them with him wherever he may retire to. Should he, however, find himself hotly pursued by our troops, I am afraid he would immediately do away with the poor prisoners, whose presence in his company would only serve to betray him wherever he went.

On the whole, therefore, I am inclined to think that, if our simple object be the liberation of the captives, our endeavour should be:

1st. To get to that portion of Theodore's frontier which is nearest to his capital, for the purpose of negotiation. This is Matammah.

2nd. These negotiations failing, to march at once upon his capital.

3rd. In the event of his retiring, to occupy his capital and the rich corn-growing and cattle-breeding districts on the shores of Lake Tsana, giving him at the same time to understand that they shall be restored to him on the liberation of the captives.

Nothing has been said about compensation, because the only adequate compensation we can have for the expense and loss of life which the expedition will entail, would be the permanent occupation of the whole of Abyssinia. In the event of Theodore's taking the lives of the captives, and also eluding our efforts to catch and punish him, it would then be for the British Government and nation to decide what should be done. Our Government has already declared its policy for the future as being, to " withdraw as much as possible from Abyssinian engagements, Abyssinian alliances, and British interference in Abyssinia ;" but it is a great question whether, before this Abyssinian affair is settled, it may not have to adopt a very different policy. Events may take such a turn as to necessarily imply an occupation for months, or even years, and then the question may come to be discussed as to whether Abyssinia itself should not be annexed to our dominions in the East, as our only amends for the trouble and expense we should then have incurred. The general impression at present is that Abyssinia is a country not worth having, but I will venture to predict that this will not be the view held by the European members of the expedition immediately the Abyssinian highlands are reached. The first impression of our countrymen on attaining the high plateau will be one of astonishment and delight. So prevalent is the idea that the whole of Central Africa is either a sandy waste or a wilderness of jungle, that our troops themselves will scarcely be open to any other view until their own experience convinces them of the immense mistake. The inconveniences they will have to put up with on the hot burning coast, and on the first portion of the march, will if anything tend to confirm their prejudices; so that their wonder will be so much the greater, when, passing through the purgatory (not to use a worse term) of the lowlands, they emerge into the paradise above. They will then find that this Africa, whose very name is a synonym for barrenness and malaria, really possesses within its broad surface tracts of beauty, of fertility, and of healthiness combined, which no other districts (I say it advisedly) either in the New or Old World can surpass. Nor will the impression be received by them alone; through them it will be ultimately felt by the British nation.

The next feeling of the army after that of surprise at the richness of the country will be one of sorrow, approaching to disgust, to see this fair portion of God's earth occupied by a race who are blind to its value, and have not enough sense to make use of the natural riches lying almost at their very doors. As the intelligent British soldier picks up on his march specimens of coal and ironstone, or takes his noon-day rest beneath some giant tree of the forest, he will see in this country a field for future colonization, and he will hardly fail to convey his impressions on friends at home, many of whom find it a life's struggle to get their daily bread. A country that, between its high mountain plateaux and low-lying valleys, is capable of yielding all the productions of temperate and tropical lands, and which is at the same time thinly populated by a race destined, apparently, to exterminate itself, must offer immense advantages to the settler.

That conquest and colonization would have been the policy adopted by us in a case like this one hundred or even fifty years since, nobody can doubt; but the impression now is, that the time for English conquests is gone by. But, though the general wisdom of this policy may not be called in question, ought we not to

make an exception in a case of this kind? Here we
have one of the richest and most fertile provinces on
the face of the globe, in every way adapted, by the
coolness of the climate and the readiness of approach
from the sea, for the purpose of European colonization
and enterprise; the key, one might almost say, by
reason of its healthiness, to the magnificent lake districts of Central Africa; and this country is occupied
by a set of people not very far removed from savages,
who, by the ill-treatment of our countrymen, have
necessitated an expedition, the cost of which will be
felt for years by the British nation. In these circumstances, should we not be justified in holding the
country permanently, in order that by that means we
may have some amends for the trouble at which we
have been? Surely, no European nation would call
in question our right. Indeed, so far from this being
the case, other nations will probably think the less of
us if we do not do so. Had "la grande nation" such a
splendid opportunity, they would assuredly not let it
slip through their fingers, judging from their policy
with regard to a comparatively barren Algeria. And
as for Turkey and Egypt, who have for centuries made
a claim upon Abyssinia, this claim has never been

recognised by Europe, no more than it has had any foundation in justice. And yet Egypt is so convinced of the importance of Abyssinia, that she would probably willingly pay all the expenses of our expedition if we would allow her to annex it.

But as the public mind is not at present prepared for a policy of this kind, we may conclude that, if our object in the liberation of our countrymen be immediately attained, we shall at once retire from the country, and leave it to its fate. That amount of protection which, as a powerful Christian nation towards a weaker one, we have hitherto given to Abyssinia, will then be almost certainly withdrawn, and from whatever quarter her future enemies may come, she need not look to us for assistance against them. The principal enemies of Christian Abyssinia are the Egyptians on the north, and the Gallas on the south. Both of these are Mohammedans, and both have been slowly but steadily progressing, each in their own direction, until the distance which separates them is now, in the Wollo Gallas round Magdala and Arab tribes on the Atbara, little more than 150 miles. The withdrawal of our sympathy and the possible weakening of the country consequent on our invasion will no doubt give fresh impulse to the aggressions of both these powers, and the result will be that, unless some European power intervene, in the course of a few years we may behold Galla and Arab exchanging their "salaams" on the shores of Lake Tsana, and rejoicing over the ruins of Christian Abyssinia. We should then see the sons of the present generation of Abyssinians, instead of wielding the spear and sword of their fathers, carrying the long *shibouk* at the heels of the Moslem merchant of Cairo and Stamboul, while the copper-coloured daughters of Makada, instead of bearing sturdy warriors to their lords, would grace the harems of the Turk. This result would not, it is true, be brought about without a sea of blood having first been shed, for Abyssinia, whose children are at least brave, would not tamely submit to the conqueror. But, although their resistance might defer for a while their entire subjection, Egypt, with all the advantages which European war-appliances and discipline would give her, must eventually triumph.

The last chance which Abyssinia had of maintaining her independence was in her acceptance of Theodore; and in rejecting him she has rejected her only saviour. He understood the situation, and felt that in the mighty power of his own will he possessed what would meet it;

but the elements of discord were too great in the nation to allow of union, and so he failed. Strength of will blinded his reason, otherwise he might have seen that *Habesh* could never be united. *Habesh* means a *mixture*, and is applied to the variety of races of which the nation is composed, and in this very variety consists its weakness. The fusion is not yet complete, if it ever will be. The Agow, the Amhara, the Galla, the Shangalla, the Jew, and the Arab still preserve to a certain extent their identity, and though united into one apparent nation, it is simply by mixture, like that of several powders in which the grains remain intact, and not like the complete union of two or more liquids.

It has been said above that the absorption of Abyssinia by Egypt, and the triumph of Mohammedanism over this last remnant of Christian power in Africa, will inevitably be the result of our determination not to interfere further in the affairs of that country, *if no other European power intervene.* But is there no other nation of Europe who will extend the ægis of its protection over the Christians of Habesh? Assuredly there is. The same power that has stood forward as the protector of the Maronites of Mount Lebanon will not refuse its support to the Christians of Ethiopia. This power is France. We would not dogmatically assert that Napoleon has at present any definite design of occupying Abyssinia, but there is no doubt but that many influential Frenchmen, especially amongst the clergy, would urge such a course on the French government, if a good excuse for carrying it out were found. And what better one could be wished than the approaching closing in on Abyssinia of those Arab and Galla Mohammedans who already surround it on all sides? The cry would then be raised that Christianity and humanity alike demand the rescue of a Christian nation from threatened destruction by fanatic and slave-dealing Moslems. And there is little doubt but that "the Eldest Son of the Church" would listen to an appeal of this kind when made in favour of a country that is key *number two* to that Red Sea which is the Englishman's high road to the East. Apart from this there is enough in the physical advantages of this African Switzerland to make interference tempting, and we must not suppose that the shameful ignorance which prevails in England with regard to Abyssinia is shared to the same extent by our neighbours over the Channel. For every Englishman and Protestant who have visited Abyssinia there have been ten

Frenchmen and Roman Catholics, and the works of travel which have been written on this subject in French are far more numerous, if not more trustworthy, than those which we possess. The French nation and Government therefore have formed a far juster estimate of the value of Abyssinia than we have; and should France ever have the incentive which before this "Abyssinian Question" is settled England may possess, we may be assured she will not have any scruples as to *her* day for conquest having gone by.